The Taming of Genghis

The Taming of Genghis

RONALD STEVENS

ISBN 978-0-88839-700-3

Cataloging in Publication Data

Stevens, Ronald, 1902–1994
The taming of Genghis / Ronald Stevens.

ISBN 978-0-88839-700-3

1. Stevens, Ronald, 1902–1994. 2. Falconers—Great Britain—Biography. 3. Genghis (Gyrfalcon). 4. Gyrfalcon—Training—Great Britain. 5. Falconry—Great Britain. 6. Human-animal relationships. I. Title.

SK321.S75 2010 799.2'32092 C2010-901276-3

Printed in South Korea — PACOM

Production & cover design: Ingrid Luters
Illustrations: C.F. Tunnicliffe

Published simultaneously in Canada and the United States by

HANCOCK HOUSE PUBLISHERS LTD.
19313 Zero Avenue, Surrey, BC Canada V3S 9R9
(604) 538-1114 Fax (604) 538-2262

HANCOCK HOUSE PUBLISHERS
1431 Harrison Avenue, Blaine, WA, USA 98230-5005
(604) 538-1114 Fax (604) 538-2262

Website: **www.hancockhouse.com**
Email: **sales@hancockhouse.com**

To
the Squires
and
the Parsons

An account of adventures and discoveries
in the training of a
GYRFALCON
Hierofalco rusticolus

CHAPTER I

A lake, a mountain and the sea beyond. The sky, so blue in the transient smiles of an Arctic summer, so leaden and lowering at most other times. Against this background Genghis had his home.

I was to know the lake well and the mountain, too, or such of it as the driving mists allowed me to see. Anyway I could not see much because the biting wind blew and blew and blew the tears into my eyes and down my nose so that it blew me into snivelling irritability. And it was cold. It was so cold and miserable that nothing on earth would have lured me to that far northern land other than the hope of being able to put a hand over a gyrfalcon, such as Genghis.

My first sight of him was in the nest, or eyrie, which was in a steep cliff at the foot of the mountain. To get to it my companions had let me down on a rope. Being no mountaineer I did not enjoy the descent and there was no mercy in the wind. Every time my toe probed for a foothold the loosened earth flew upwards on the updraught, like smoke from a kindling, so that it caught my face and tried to blind me. It seemed that everything was telling me I should not be there, that I was unwanted and unwelcome, but not quite everything said that for there were shy smiles in the little flowers that clung in the rocks' interstices out of the wind, and, as I went down, the singing voices of seals, softly dolorous, were borne fitfully to me on the wind from the sea, and from the black waters of the lake below, the weird, contemptuous laugh of a redthroated diver appropriately hailed my adventure.

In that descent was the exciting discovery of a world of topsyturveydom where the dimensions were in reverse. I clung to the massive cliff face where the illusion of security made it seem like a floor with the force of gravity seeming to pull me the wrong way. Where the rock receded inwards I was pulled outwards, away from it. It was like trying to land with waving feet desperately trying to contact the earth. And when I approached the rock ledge, on which the eyrie was, it was like dropping in on somebody through an open upstairs window because of an absurd inability to walk in on him from below. And that person could not have gaped more in surprise than did the two young falcons at my entry. It was something unusual. So unusual that one of them, the male or tiercel, in his fright leapt off the eyrie. Horror struck me for what I had done, for that bird was too young to fly. With a sheer drop of a couple of hundred feet his tender young body with the flight feathers only in bud was bound to be pulped on the scree down below. So I thought, but wonder and thankfulness filled me as his weak wings sustained him in faltering flight all the way down, to bring him in safety to one of the basal boulders at the foot of the cliff.

I looked at his sister who was rolled on her side six feet away from me, her wide-open talons stretched upwards towards me in a gesture of warding off any further harm I might do. Her mouth was open in apprehension and her eyes blazed with the will to fight. How utterly wild she looked! And how wildly beautiful the place! Across that valley in which snow still lay was another row of cliffs and from these hung huge icicles like rows of giants' swords. From the platform of the eyrie, on which in all probability no man before me had ever stood, I faced that cruel arctic solitude, feeling like an outcast from the world.

From below, out of the valley's deep shadow, the updraught was numbing my body and my senses as if it were the chill breath of death. I had seen all I wanted to, and more, so I pulled away on the rope in my ascent, being anxious to regain the top of the cliff before all feeling had gone out of my hands.

Willing hands pulled me over the last bit, there was friendliness in their strong grasp, in those hands of Arni, Starri and Sverrir my companions. I stood among them not as a sightseer, a tourist, but as somebody who was doing something with them. In other parts of the world where my hawk hunting and ornithological pursuits had taken me it was always the same, that feeling of oneness with the natives because we were sharing something in which we had a common interest.

The loneliness I had previously felt vanished on rejoining my companions and together, on a roundabout trail in that wild region, we descended to the foot of the cliff to make sure that the nestling had suffered no harm. We found him, squatting and humped like a huge avian toad, his head thrust forward menacingly towards us. The white down sprouted all over him between his growing feathers, giving him an untidy, ugly appearance, but no, not ugly really, because how can gawky youth look ugly when it is covered with the promise of elegance to come?

So we left him there on the rock, and his sister in the

eyrie; we left them both to the care of the parent birds for I did not want to take a callow nestling home but a bird fully grown, one that had experience in flying, that had already learnt how to prey for itself.

On a previous occasion I had taken a nestling and in no time it had become wonderfully tame and confiding, but its tameness was of the aggressive, rude, over-familiar, disrespectful kind. He refused to take his training seriously and when I tried to persuade him to fly at grouse he mostly flew in the opposite direction, and he used to return to me in his own good time, to suit his convenience and not mine, meanly taking advantage of the fact that he had no need to exert himself to catch a grouse when I, the poor old falconer, was bound to give him food when he chose to ask for it. In common with all hawks taken in the nestling stage his manners were appalling. He fed greedily and snatched the tit-bits from me, not caring whether he bit or scratched the fingers that proffered them. His behaviour was like that of a spoilt child of the nursery.

Peregrines are the same when taken from the eyrie but their gaucherie can be cured by turning them out to hack, that is to say by allowing them to fly about completely at liberty for a month from the time they learn to fly. During this time the falconer puts food down for them every day, and they help themselves to it until they learn to prey for themselves by which time they have become as unapproachable as any wild hawk. After they have been trapped, and training begins, it will be found that the winds of freedom have refined their earlier raw immaturity so that in their relationship with the falconer they have become gentle and well-mannered. Unfortunately such treatment is ineffective against the nestling gyrfalcon's bad manners because at hack, during her days of liberty, she refuses to become wild, having the intelligence to know that from the falconer she has nothing to fear, indeed in her boisterous affection she shows a good-natured contempt for him, being too ready to regard her training as an excuse for playfulness. With this in mind I had decided that my next gyr would not be lifted from the nest so that I would again be subjected to another demand for a sheltered existence under me. Instead of that I had planned to catch it well beyond its infancy, when its schooling was finished and it had learnt how to prey for itself. It would be a refreshing experience to have a proud and independent gyr to train in place of a frivolous one. That is why we left Genghis and his sister by the lake for a while longer in the care of their parents, so that they would learn to fly over the mountain and the sea beyond. And we wished that their flying would not be restricted by enclosing walls of mists but that the sun of an arctic summer would yet welcome them up to the freedom and light of spacious blue skies.

It is the way of falcons with their young to teach them to fly and to hunt until the time arrives when the immature birds can conduct their own lives, and that stage is reached within a little more than a month of their leaving the eyrie. Then the family party is broken up and the old birds drive their young away to fend for themselves. But before the young gyrs would fly away on their own independent ways into the world we should catch one of them, preferably the tiercel, for so we had planned. Accordingly day after day, week after week, I continued to keep the family party under observation, sometimes in company with my Nordic friends, sometimes alone.

In those regions of the midnight sun the absence of clear-cut day and night makes a person careless of the hour, particularly when mist and cloud obscure the sun and so add to the confusion. There were times when I found myself out on the cliffs, at what should have been the dawn, when the land at the back of me was hidden by mist so that the ocean was seemingly all around. Thus it appeared to lie, an endless, timeless stretch of water. On the few occasions when there was no wind the sea ran oily smooth and the underlying swell raised rafts of eider duck to catch my eye. In all that encompassing vast solitude there was a pristine beauty in the soft lights that lit with delicate colours the steaming sea. Such tranquillity was there that thought, which at other times lost its vigour in the cruel winds and got damped down by fog, soared into the filtering, early sunshine. It had a startling clarity for it was without desires and found nothing to analyse nor problems to solve. In its freedom it could find but three words—In the Beginning, in the Beginning.

Finally the day came when I judged it was opportune to catch him. He had killed a ptarmigan. I lowered my field glasses, slung them on my back and started to hurry over the half mile of country that separated him from me. On my approach he flew off, leaving the dead ptarmigan behind. Using this as bait I set the trap and hurried away. I had not gone a couple of hundred yards before he was back again. Still walking away I watched over my shoulder the blob on the ground that was he, but when that blob twinkled with flickering wings I spun round knowing that he was caught. Then I ran towards him with the intention of getting him out of the trap as quickly as possible before he should break a feather. Within twenty yards I slowed down into a strolling walk and strolled up to him. Then calmly and unhurriedly I took him out of the trap, nursing what little hope there might be of his disassociating me from his being caught and associating me with rescue. I had him out of the trap well within the time limit for not a feather on his body was injured, and after mentally apologizing for our graceless introduction I vowed that the same hands that had closed round him in capture would in gentleness carry him on to a new life in which we should find equal pleasure. It is written that man shall have dominion over the fowls of the air, but Genghis is not of the kind to suffer dominion. I asked for partnership. How generously this lord of the air gave me his share of it can be appreciated from the story that follows.

CHAPTER II

Now that you know the origins of Genghis the gyrfalcon I can take you and him to my home in the wildest part of the Welsh Marches.

It is the early morning of a beautiful summer's day and I am on my way to the hawk mews. Before leaving the house I had my pre-breakfast cup of tea, and stepping out into the pale sunshine, which as yet has only a hint of warmth in it, is just like marching out into life itself. From the lake below that winds through the park, river fashion, comes the vociferation of waterfowl which in its variety imitates every instrument in a grand orchestra. Thus the bugles of Canada geese, the violins of carolinas, the penny whistles of tree-ducks, the flutes of black-necked swans, the French horns of bar-headed geese, and so many more, fill the air like a vast tuning-up before the curtain of the day is raised.

During those early days after his capture Genghis was like a lost soul, being lifted out of one life and not yet re-cast in the next. I remember so well that particular morning when I was with him in the cool gloom of the mews. Raised to the level of my shoulder on his perch he was a proud, heroic figure in the centre of that room. The hood that he wore put him, for the time being, in the shadow of captivity. There was as yet no small voice of freedom to penetrate his circle of consciousness.

That is how I saw him. On my entry he drew his head back and slightly opened his beak, being fully ready, even in that subjected condition, to fight me to his last breath. Stripped of everything that he loved in life he had nothing left except naked defiance. I could take everything away from him, but not that. Did I feel sorry for him? Can one feel sorry for something that is fit almost for idolatry?

He and I alone in that room. I cannot write 'we', for in that psychological atmosphere there was not the smallest hint of company. On the one hand was a creature in its pristine splendour, and on the other a man who had set himself the difficult task of training it, and who would not let the bird go free again until he had won its confidence. As yet I could not lay the lightest finger-tip on its breast feathers without provoking an angry hiss. It must drive me away and demand that I keep away.

Not liking the silence and the chilliness that had the mews in their grip I began to pace up and down so as to instil some semblance of life into the place. Up and down, up and down I paced with measured tread. Not only for my sake but for his I paced up and down, hoping that my rhythmic footfalls would fall in concord with the beating of his heart. Thus I marched into the very smallest of beginnings of unity with him. I paced up and down. It was difficult for me to stop because something had to be done in the way of humble approach to his proud, independent spirit and I was doing it. In imagination I was walking towards him over the vast spiritual desert that divided us. After half an hour he ceased to turn his head in following me, by hearing, from one side of the room to the other. He stood motionless, the burnished grey of his plumage making him appear as though cast in metal.

As I paced up and down little sounds began to come up from below. Someone was chopping wood. The staccato *chop, chop, chop* joined the tapping of my feet on the stone floor. Someone passed by, his boots crunching the gravel. Then I heard the sharp, high notes of children's voices. All these sounds came up the hill and into the mews, like little winged darts, to pin themselves on Genghis's frozen composure, but he did not move. Later on, at about lunch-time, everything went quiet again down below, so quiet that I could hear the inner poundings in my ears, and still he remained absolutely motionless. As I continued to pace up and down conscious thoughts drained out of my head and a dream-like state came over me. The mews became a temple, set on a hill; the hawk raised high on its perch, was an idol, a Nordic god, forcibly borne away from its realms of snow and ice, and I was its appointed priest. When the wood-chopping started again down below it was the tap-tapping of the tom-toms of tribesmen bent on a rite of propitiation.

The time arrived when something else had to be done. My hours of pacing had quietened him into sullen impassivity. My vigil had not tired me, rather the reverse, for I had been walking much as a sleep-walker does. I was entranced and it needed some effort to rouse myself, and, as on all such occasions, I waited for some signal, as though waiting to be told just the right moment for beginning the next stage of the proceedings. When a cock crowed outside I suddenly stopped. Now was the time.

Taking up the leather gauntlet I drew it over my left hand and looked at Genghis. I went up to him and on my approach he knew at once that I was about to do something which he believed threatened his security. He drew his head back and opened his beak in angry apprehension. When I put my gloved fist under his tail and lightly against the back of his legs he still kept his open beak directed towards my face, sensing that it was in the head of his captor and not the hands that potential menace had its origin. I put a little more pressure on the back of his legs and the nervous reaction made him step back. He was on the fist, hissing and puffing out all his body feathers in bristling defiance, ready to strike out with beak and clawed foot at anything almost before it was within his reach. Every time my foot came to the ground as I slowly walked forward he threw his head still farther back so that it jerked violently to my footfalls, but he quickly dropped back into sullen resignation, and I resumed my pacing up and down, carrying him on my fist. I had no intention of allowing him to smoulder again in impassivity. Progress demanded that I must now keep him fully alive to my presence and this through touch. To ask him to bear the feel of my hand would be asking too much, it had to be something more impersonal. He would bear the feel of a breeze against him because its touch would be a friendly one. He might endure the flight feather of a goose being gently laid on him. I produced one and with its tip touched him on the breast with little more weight in the contact than one of the millions of snowflakes that would have descended on him in his Arctic homeland. But he knew the difference and with every fibre of his being fought off these advances as though they were yet another of captivity's links in a chain with which I sought to encircle him.

How could I convey to him that far from pushing him down deeper into captivity I wanted to bring him up out of it? The time would come when he would begin to appreciate my good intentions, but for the present we were in active disagreement. He wanted to escape to freedom and, leaving me far behind and far below, continue on his own independent way. I wanted to lead him into freedom, but along my way so that I could enjoy a falconer's privilege of sharing with him, on the surface at least, his own world, the world of flight.

Stroking his breast and lightly touching his wing butts I strove, through the medium of the goose feather, to put something of myself into him. For some time he resisted these attentions as though, at every touch, the quill burnt him, but after about an hour he began to show signs that he was becoming accustomed to the feel of it. I could then stroke him on the breast and he would do no more than open his beak in a gesture of distrust which had replaced the former, stronger emotion of defiance. But when I stroked him on the back he turned his head and opened his beak wider, pointing it in an upward direction over his wing butt. This display of stronger objection indicated an aversion, common to all birds even when they are tame, to being touched on the back. When the human touch is against the breast a bird still instinctively feels free to escape it by upward flight, but lay a hand over its back and it will be frightened because it will feel held to earth.

By the time I put Genghis back on his perch some small beginnings of progress had been made. I stepped out into the bright sunlight. It was late afternoon of a fine day. Chinese water-deer were emerging from their tunnels in the shadows to graze across the park, cranes danced down by the edge of the lake, peacocks paraded their magnificence over the wide lawns below.

But when I returned to the mews an hour or two later anyone would have thought that Genghis had profited nothing from the time I had previously spent with him. He drew himself back and hissed and raised all his feathers in anger as I took him on the fist. Nevertheless all this boiling over did not last as long as it did on the previous occasion; soon he subsided into his former immobility while I paced up and down, carrying him on the fist.

He had refused all food since capture. This would do him no physical harm because these arctic falcons are accustomed to fasting for days at a time when long spells of blizzard or fog make it impossible for them to hunt. But a beginning had to be made and I was determined that this day he should feed. I sat down and held a piece of meat over his feet, hoping that the feel of it would awaken appetite.

Some people believe that birds of prey have the sense of smell well developed. All the ones that I have handled have never provided any evidence of this; indeed quite the contrary. Hundreds of time I have had a tame hawk on my fist, hooded and ravenously hungry, with a steaming piece of raw flesh from a freshly killed bird held under her beak. Never was any sign given of her knowing that it was there, not until it touched her feet when she would instantly put her head down to feed. If birds of prey have no sense of smell it surely is very doubtful whether any other kind of bird has it.

For an hour Genghis paid not the slightest attention to the food. When I stroked his feet with it he did nothing more than half open his beak in half-hearted protest. Later he got tired even of that little gesture. Through his immobility his resentment only faintly glowed. Was I to let his burning resentment cool off into nothing better than dour moodiness? With a pair of tweezers holding a tit-bit of meat I touched him on the beak. That drew an angry hiss from him and before he closed his beak again I had put the bit of meat into his mouth, hoping that the taste of food would bring new thoughts into his head. I thought that possibly he might swallow the tenth piece but he just went on flinging them all away contemptuously

To him they were not worth a second's consideration. His pride he refused to swallow and he had abysmal contempt for man's trying to garnish it with juicy bits of meat. His demand for freedom sublimated his body's need of sustenance. I might as well have offered him pebbles as those bits of meat. Very well. No need for discouragement. I was not surprised. I would not have had him any different, being so glad to accept him for just what he was.

What would you have done? Removed his hood and the furniture of captivity and let him fly away? I could have done the same. Then you and I could have enjoyed watching his regained freedom? No we could not because he would be gone in a flash and we should never see him again. We could go to the far north and study gyrfalcons in their natural environment and return with notes and photographs. To me that would be like grasping at a shadow. I want the gyrfalcon, and in time I would hope and expect that, far from resenting me, it would enjoy my company. But I want a gyrfalcon only on the understanding that after winning its confidence I put it on the wing again, so that it will be not only free to fly but free to fly away from me if it wants to.

At that moment Genghis's desire for his own independent freedom was 99·99 per cent. His confidence in me was 00·01 per cent. But in time the measure of those emotions would be just about reversed. This would be possible only through gentleness and leading him the right way.

At that moment there was only one course open to me to get him to feed. I would have to hold his hand, or rather his foot which is his hand as well. So very gently I took his left foot with my bare right hand and put it between the thumb and first finger of my gloved left one, holding it there just sufficiently firmly so that he could not withdraw it. But do not make the mistake of thinking this was to be an affectionate approach. I was relying on something quite different. Instantly he was fully awake to what he regarded as an unwarranted liberty on my part. His pride and dignity were offended, for I knew that we had reached the stage where his lessening fear of me would allow them to burn the more brightly. Take your defiling hand off me! So his fury spoke, and he tore savagely at the meat because, though dead flesh, it was flesh all the same and the only available, my own living hand being protected by the glove. He made pieces of meat fly all over the room, they hit me in the face and lodged in the folds of my clothing. I had to blink to keep them out of my eyes. Then O! Splendid. Splendid. They were going down his throat, lubricated by the principle that enemies were to be eaten up, but, afterwards, swallowed because they tasted good. On that discovery he tightened his feathers which had been puffed out in anger and gave himself up to the raw pleasure of eating, eating, eating. He tore off great hunks and strained in swallowing them, wheezing and gasping to get them down. Then suddenly he stopped. I had let go of his foot which he had at once mechanically withdrawn so that, standing once again squarely on the fist, he was back where he was, in full possession of all his faculties, rigid, proud and dignified. I had hoped that on releasing his foot he would continue feeding, but in this I was disappointed though not surprised. I must again unbalance him, physically and mentally, to bring into action again his biting anger. So I did, and he continued to feed, by then not so much in anger as in annoyance which quickly changed to the simple satisfaction of satisfying his hunger. Fear, fury, sullenness. These props to his wild independence were surely coming down while I was stepping over them and coming in to meet him. Soon he would tolerate me. Later he would like me.

At that moment he was thinking very little of me but a lot of his food. He was scarcely aware of his foot's being held. I continued to hold it lightly, happy in the satisfaction of seeing the good, red, rawmeat going down his gullet. Some hawks would have replaced fear by timidity, eating their food in tiny mouthfuls. Such rarely turn out to be good hawks when trained. It was already obvious that Genghis was not of that kind. He approached everything massively in a wholesale, single-minded manner, and how I liked him for that!

I let him go on feeding until he had taken nearly three-quarters of a crop, then I released his foot and he stopped. Quietly I put him on his perch for the night. I did not stroke him with the feather because he might have hissed and I wanted nothing discordant to break his last agreeable impression. It was deeply satisfying to see the pleasant bulge on his crop. He looked almost at peace when I left.

CHAPTER III

Lately I have been carrying Genghis on the fist as I go about the estate. He must be getting well used to the feel of the fist by now. I can stroke him with the feather, even over his back, without his hissing. It is desirable now to move about among people to accustom him to the sound of their voices. He already knows mine well enough. This morning I took him round to the kennels so that he could hear the dogs' barking. He listened to the noise of agricultural machinery and in a blacksmith's shop the noise of hammer blows rained all over him, but, except for his head, he hardly moved at all. There was no visible evidence to show that he was in the least affected by all these alien sounds, but I would have given much to have known what went on in his head under the hood he was wearing. I feel immensely proud of him when showing him off to people. To see him on the fist, every line of him unbending, conjures up in the mind's eye some splendid savage chieftain in the market place in ancient Rome. But here the analogy ends because he will never be for sale. Never will he fall into the hands of anyone who, through ignorance, callousness or wanton sentimentality, would cruelly misuse him.

I visited the mews again after tea, calling out to him on

my approach. After my absence he still draws his head back a little and gives one hiss as the glove contacts his feet. He still hisses on the first feel of the goose feather against his wing-butts and back. After that he hisses no more for the rest of the session.

By now he feels so much a part of me when on the fist, because of his familiarity with the feel of it, that I had hoped his decreasing fear would put him in the mood for feeding without any of the previous persuasion that had been necessary yesterday. In this, however, I was disappointed. I sat with him all the way up to supper-time with meat on the glove under his feet. He knew it was there but his pride would not let him bend down to it. After supper I was compelled in the end to hold his foot again and he attacked the food. After a couple of mouthfuls his fury disappeared and he ate as though he had only been waiting all the time for this persuasion to lead him out of the rut of his ill-humour. So entirely did he abandon himself to the pleasure of satisfying his hunger that anyone seeing him at that moment would probably have been deceived in the belief that he was receiving encouragement through my holding his foot.

I was talking to him quietly all the time in the deep gloom of the mews, for it had become dark. Still talking I let go his foot and to my relief and joy he continued to feed as freely as if there were nothing else between him and earth and sky.

The whole garden was quietening down for the night, lights were coming up from the Hall and to them I was walking. The moon was up and so much of its light was enclosed in the small courtyard that it made me want to enter it. As I did so I was aware of much repose between its walls and I realized that although I had stood there many times before I was now on the threshold of discovery. For one thing the fountain in the middle of the circular lily pond had never looked like that before. It was the simplest kind of fountain that sent its water up in a single jet, not the spray type which would have been entirely out of keeping with the lovely simplicity of the place. But by day it was just an ordinary fountain, sometimes it was less than that when the feed pipe got stopped up. This night, however, it was running free and seemingly out of control because its playful water spurted up into moonlight and sight could not measure it. The sparkles on the surface of the pond played on their own with nothing visible to connect them with the water beating down. From far above its bowl and all around, out of the night, moonlight and shadow, and from out of the peace that covered all, its running, bubbling and pattering let it be known that tonight the fountain was liberated. Both mentally and visually I tried to lay the fountain's nocturnal frivolity. I looked and looked up and up but the riddle defeated me. Behind the mystery the lively waters played and only hearing received their spilling.

I could not go. There never was such a place in daytime. It was an experience that I should never have again, for if I deliberately sought it another time its second revelation would not be quite the same.

Then there was the garden-party at our squire's place for raising money for the Hunt's funds. Everything was superbly organized. Scores of little tea-tables were dotted about in the shady parts of the wide lawns and under an ancient mulberry tree an orchestra was playing Mozart's 'Eine Kleine Nachtmusik', the Seranade in G major, which so exactly matched the prettily formal occasion. I strolled about among the well-dressed people in this very English garden with Genghis on my fist, frequently explaining that as a representative of his species he is a gyrfalcon and that gyrtiercel refers to his sex. He gave me distinction; nothing else about me ever could. I passed from one group to another receiving praises on his behalf until I grew a little shy in his reflected glory. At a tea-table I rested my gauntleted fist on my left thigh, half turning to talk to an Australian lady on my right, waving the goose quill while I was talking and quietly stroking the hawk with it when I was not. But it was she who did most of the talking.

Having no liking for social occasions I was glad to escape the garden-party. Talking for talking's sake tires me more than anything else on earth, so that it was with relief and thankfulness that I addressed myself to Genghis again that evening. To my delight he seized the meat the moment it was given him. It was more than that offering that I laid at his feet, so that when he fed freely without my having to hold his foot I saw in his acceptance his first willing co-operation with me. He now no longer regards me as an out-and-out enemy.

Such good effect has all the carrying in public places had on him that he continued to feed when two people entered the mews and spoke to me. I was startled into some annoyance at their entry because it was as unexpected as it was unwelcome. It is always understood at the house that when I am closeted with a hawk in the mews I am not at home to callers. In this case, however, the butler had used his discretion because one of these men is an old friend and he, knowing my ways, more or less pushed through the defences and here he was. I was relieved and pleased to see him but nevertheless, supporting myself on our friendship, told him in a few words just what the position was; that I had recently returned from the far north with a gyrtiercel and, after some trouble, had, as he saw, succeeded in persuading the hawk to feed of his own accord. Would he mind very much if he, and the gentleman he had brought along to meet me, allowed me a quarter of an hour so that I could finish up in the mews. If they would go down to the lake I would join them there at the earliest possible moment, and we could show his friend the waterfowl and would probably be in time to join Dick at the birds' evening feed. My friend said he would do that and off they went.

Genghis went on feeding while I felt just a little guilty at excusing myself like that. All the same, manning a hawk in the early stages does call for concentration and I could not have done the job properly if my attention had been divided by making pleasantries to visitors. I hoped that the excuse and the put-on deprecatory smile had met the situation but I could not be sure. On the realization of that an uncomfortable feeling came over me that my friend did not noticeably show any sympathetic understanding as he turned to go. I did not allow this disquiet to be conveyed to Genghis through hurried movements, but as soon as I had put him on the perch I lost no time in following after the two visitors. When he had finished his meal and while still on the fist he had delighted me by rousing. Rousing is the loosening out of all the feathers and the vigorous shaking of them all back into place again. A hawk only does this when contented so that was why I was so pleased. It probably added to my affability when I caught up with the two men. But my friend was not his usual easy, pleasant self. He had something on his mind and I knew what that was. Nevertheless I put on a show of cordiality hoping to make him believe that I was insensitive to his mood. Under those circumstances it was easy for me to pretend that anxiety to entertain the other man chiefly occupied my thoughts and conversation.

So, as we walked round there was not a bird that came before us that escaped the fire of my lecturing on what species or sub-species it belonged to, what part of the world it came from and what its life history was. On the last my glib tongue ran on into all sorts of elaborations. I held forth on all the native beliefs and superstitions that I could think of that could possibly be tied in with the subjects of my ornithological lecture. All this I did with a challenging eye on my friend. After leaving the lake we came up through the park to the garden and all the way I was pointing out this and that, hoping, by my volubility, to convey that the quarter of an hour of my absence from them was my loss rather than theirs. When, at the end of it all, we stood inside the house I felt quite tired. My friend's friend had gone to the lavatory while my friend and I stood in the entrance hall, in silence, facing each other. What a contrast that silence was to the talk, talk, talk, chatter, chatter, chatter, that had been going on before! My friend was wearing a look on his face that conveyed to me 'Good heavens! I've never heard you talk like that before!' Then suddenly we started to laugh, not uproariously, because we did not want the other man to hear us, but in silent agony. We shook and twitched and the breath came in and out of us in sniffs, hisses and little sneezes. 'Shut up, here he comes!'

Over the question of guest entertainment I regret that I have on many occasions fallen into disfavour with people because I selfishly expect them to interpret it in the same way as I do. Because in all these things I am conscious, as I write, of your critical judgment, reader, I must confess that in this instance my own definition of entertainment is more apologetic than explanatory. The word is closely associated with hospitality, and that, as I see it, implies a warm reception into somebody else's home and the liberal provision by him of food and lodging, a Christian act of beautifully simple sincerity that blesses host and guest. Entertainment can include that but it also implies something more diverting. It means that the simple giving of hospitality is not enough—it must make a *show* of it and, if possible, add interest and amusement too. Praiseworthy motives of course, but unfortunately they so often attract the discordant element of anxiety. Anxiety on the part of the host as to whether he is putting on a good enough show, and anxiety on the guest's part as to whether he is reflecting a lively enough appreciation of it. Some people who are not as lively in wit and conversation as they would like to be are inclined to feel the strain when being entertained. To be pursued by kindness all through the day can be a nerve-racking experience for the guest. There have been times when, having gained temporary sanctuary in the bedroom assigned to me, I would have paid a soveriegn to have been allowed to rest on the settee for half an hour before changing for dinner, with a guarantee that no knock on the door would break the healing silence.

It seems that our modern world decrees that hospitality is not enough. It is not enough to allow your guest the simple enjoyment of your home, to sit at table with your wife and family, to walk in your garden, to take part in the day's uninterrupted proceedings or not, according to his ability and inclination. Above all he must be given no opportunity to be alone to form his own impressions, for you will take care of those for him. That, in my possibly mistaken judgment, is what entertainment implies; and because I refuse to impose the conventional interpretation of it as host in our own home, I sometimes disappoint a guest. My friends mostly come to stay with me when they invite themselves. They know what to expect and if they do not enjoy themselves, as I enjoy having them, they would not come again. Circumstances do sometimes, however, necessitate sending out an invitation. 'Come and stay,' I write. 'Don't expect to be entertained, but make yourself at home or regard our house as an hotel, as you like. In either case you will be most welcome.'

During the next two days Genghis did all that was required of him. When I took him up and carried him, when I stroked him and put him down, he raised no protest. On the positive side he ended up by stepping on to my fist almost with a show of eagerness. I no longer have to make him step backwards on to the fist simply through the nervous reaction that results from touching the back of his legs, for by now I only have to lift his toe for him willingly to step forward on to the glove. In this voluntary action he has gone his farthest yet to meet me.

A dentist once surprised me by saying that after a lifetime of extracting people's teeth he still feels slightly nervous when faced with this operation. I still feel slightly nervous each time I take the hood off a newly captured hawk for the first time. I was faced with this now. It was almost certain that everything would go all right, yet there was just the chance that my hand might fumble the putting on again of the hood. Or, heaven forbid! Someone might enter the mews, and then what an inpouring of disaster there would be! Just as the dentist keeps up a patter of talk to distract the patient's attention, so I talked now to Genghis, only I could not be sure who was the patient, he or I. With over-elaborate care I was preparing everything for the great unveiling, for the moment when the light of his new life would break in upon him. Not the full glare of the noonday of that brilliant future which I hoped so ardently would be his, no, nothing more than the light of a single candle. There is nothing psychologically strange I suppose in the mixing of a certain amount of superstition with the ancient art of falconry, so perhaps my semi-conscious watchfulness for signs and portents at a time like this may be allowed. I saw one now in the steady flame of the candle. It brought tranquillity to the mews from which all other light had been excluded. It sweetened the air and dispelled the chill of apprehension.

The hood that Genghis was still wearing was about to be removed. From the time of his capture it had covered his mind with darkness, the darkness of the tunnel through which he is travelling from one life to another. Only for a little time will he glimpse surroundings that will be so weirdly strange to him that he will be relieved to find himself back in the former darkness of the hood. I recalled a childhood's experience that had taken me to a fairground. Over the opening to a tunnel the word Fairyland blazed in glittering letters. I feared the darkness of that tunnel on entering it, but had become sufficiently accustomed to it, and to the noisy chariot that sped me on my way, that when the first of successive scenes of fairyland burst upon my view, revealing less of fairies than of hobgoblins, I was almost glad when the frightening sight was shut off when we re-entered the tunnel.

In this case I AM THE HIDEOUS BOGEY. He lets out a great gasp. We freeze, he and I.

This mews, this ill-lit cave that we are in—is it a tomb, the final abyss that I have dragged him down into? Its chill and silence say it is, and we ourselves are as rigid as a couple of corpses. But the candle's flame continues to burn no less steadily than it did before, and its light falls upon him and me. For the first time in his new life he sees that we are together. In the teeming sensations of his mind, through the density of amazement and awe, he is trying to grasp the meaning of me, for I have gone far beyond being his captor.

He is staring at me with an intensity that I can feel but not see. I cannot get my eyes up to his for he would see in mine more than he could bear. Falconers do not look their ramage hawks in the eye. But I can see his powerful feet with their spreading toes, their petty singles armed with eight black, needle-sharp claws curved like scimitars, and above them his mail, his breast feathers drawn tight by fearful anticipation. Above that I dare not look. As I am now, so, with downcast eyes, a heathen would contemplate his idol.

It was a strange experience, like sitting under water, with eyesight aching to come to the surface. It seemed that only by feeling their way up to his could my eyes continue to function. They suffered for their constancy and felt that they must raise themselves if they were to continue to see.

I cannot help feeling his power. The stillness becomes oppressive with the knowledge that there is not the smallest indication of what is going to happen next. Unless there is some stir or movement even my breathing will cease. My eyes break from the will, that, until this moment, has controlled them. My mind calls stop! But they have succeeded in their efforts to escape, and now nothing can prevent their looking up.

During recent days his body has begun to assume the look of tameness. At first the bird's wildness glistened in it, but now it no longer sparks to the touch. The heat of fury and resentment has cooled in it—in the body, but under cover of the hood it has been left smouldering in the head. Now that his uncovered head is exposed to the air the heat is fanned again. It blazes out of his eyes, compelling me to lower my own again.

It was only a glimpse I had of them, but in that moment I saw the change that has taken place. In the beginning, when he was captured, the look he gave me was a defensive one, of a bird defiantly not giving way before a more powerful enemy, but now his shining eyes challengingly met my own, and they drove them away. Until now he has always been subject to me, but just now I am subject to him. The next move must come from him. I surrendered the initiative to him with the removing of his hood. Up to the moment of unhooding him I had been talking to him, but the moment the hood was off I closed my mouth, being anxious to withdraw as much of my personality as possible, knowing that there would be still more than enough of its perplexities to preoccupy him.

The humble candle only feebly illumines the bareness within these four walls, yet it sheds mystery with such effect as to bring into sharp relief the great significance of the sudden psychological change that has come over my hawk and me in our relationship. In its spell the perceptions are narrowed so that I turn mentally to look back down the events that stretch into that northern journey in which capture had so suddenly diverted us from our former habits of life. I see that journey now as a dream in which this creature had come to me so intensely alive that my understanding since then has had to wrestle with it. So Genghis confronts me now. Before the intensity of his valiant gaze I do not feel the confusion of one who has much to answer for, but the embarrassment that a mortal would feel if a god had descended to look at him. What have I brought back with me? Is it a bird that I must lead, or is it a Being that has taken charge of me?

I continued to sit there—for how long I do not know—with nothing coming in from without, and nothing happening within. And all the time I knew that he was gazing at me. The feeling that he was studying me with calculating appraisal both thrilled and embarrassed me, but how much longer would it continue?

Then I heard something and everything was changed. I began to breathe the fresh air of recovery after my long submergence in the stillness. At long last Genghis had decided to accept me, because it was his feeding that I now heard. It was pure relief to feel the vibrations through my gloved fist as he pulled at the meat. Life continued after its long, chilling pause and Genghis had decided to come with me. Very, very slowly I turned my head to enjoy the sight, for the first time, of an unhooded Genghis feeding freely on my fist. He was feeding in the belief that he stood on my fist of his own free-will, though truly the poorly lighted mews was not much of a world to tempt him to escape into by flight. When he was first caught he would have fought hysterically to avoid a meeting with me like the present one. The close company of a man would have been utterly abhorrent to him. . . . But now he was in agreement with me, there was room enough in our world of small beginnings for the two of us. One lighted candle had shown him the way and he had taken it. I, too, now looked to the cosy confidence of the candle's steady flame. I needed that confidence, for very soon I should have to put the hood on him again and so take this little world away from him for another twenty-four hours.

Could I hood him without causing him to bate? A hawk bates when attempting to fly away from the fist, but as its feet are tethered by a leather leash, leaving it only a few inches of free play, it cannot escape and its attempts to do so only make it hang from the fist. It can quickly regain the fist of course but the incident is an unfortunate one because it upsets the hawk physically and mentally if only for a moment. It can happen once or twice and the bird will think that it is nothing more than an accident, but repetition will create an impression of restriction which it will associate with the falconer. That is why the falconer takes such special care to prevent his hawk's bating. For this very reason I have darkened the mews, knowing that there would be far less likelihood of a bate in dim candle-light than in the daylight.

Although I have taken hawks along the course of their training, up to the time of their flying, without a single bate, I still feel a little nervous when it comes to re-hooding one for the first time after capture, as I was now about to do with Genghis. It must be done deftly and lightly, for if, during his training, he receive from me one heavy-handed touch he would never forget nor forgive, and this story would end with his flying away from me, for ever.

As his feeding continued his confidence grew, and that enabled me, almost imperceptibly, to move my right hand, containing the hood, up to the glove on my left on which he stood. I moved it only when he had his head down on the meat in my fist, and kept it still when he looked up. When it all but touched the glove he straightened himself up, realizing that I intended to do something. This was the moment I wanted. I moved my hand up to the level of his breast. He drew his head back and opened his beak to hiss in apprehension. Then, to divert his attention from the hood, I looked him in his eyes that blazed again as if fanned by dawning fear. He was so intent on looking, with angry questioning, into mine, that he scarcely saw the hood that slid under his lower mandible with no more pressure than the touch of a feather. When it came up before his eyes he put his head back defiantly, and that gave me my chance to complete the movement. I extinguished the raw splendour of those eyes. The hood was on.

I had him hooded before he had finished his meal, while the act of feeding engaged his attention. Even then there had been just the psychological moment for the hooding act which, in itself, called for exact timing. In manning a hawk the whole performance would break down without unerring judgment and sense of rhythm. An inexperienced person would have about as much chance of success in all this as I should have in a piano concerto, being unable to perform on the piano. But my claim to be able to tame a bird as wild as a hawk carries no boast because having been a falconer all my life it would be surprising if it were otherwise. Nor is such skill as I have any reward for patient endeavour. I practise the art simply because I like it.

So Genghis was hooded again, he had re-entered the dark tunnel through which his train of thoughts is travelling from one life to another. From now his glimpses of the new country will become increasingly frequent. It will become less strange to him, as, with the hood's removal, he sees more and more of it.

I had hoped that on his being hooded again he would continue his feeding with the hood on. That really would have been the apex of achievement. It would have indicated a splendid recovery on his part from the shock of his recent experience. In my intense desire for such a crowning reward I found my voice again.

'Go on, go on! Eat, eat!' I urged him, but he would not. I could have held his foot but the time for that sort of persuasion had passed for ever. Then I recalled with gratitude the events of the evening. After all, we had made a good beginning.

CHAPTER IV

Genghis had by now arrived at the stage when he would put his head down to feel for food on my taking him on to the fist. I would let him commence his feed with the hood on. When I took it off he would continue feeding without a break, without so much as looking round the mews. I would hood him again before his meal was quite finished, the object being to accustom him to the feel of the hood's being put on while his attention was occupied in the enjoyment of eating, for to have hooded him after the completion of his meal would have been psychologically the wrong moment, for if repeated it would soon lead him to associate the presentation of the hood with the end of a meal. That is why I always made sure that there was still some meat left over for him to enjoy after putting the hood on him again.

After giving him three feeds by candle-light I dared to open the mews door just a very little for his next feed, allowing no more illumination from daylight than what he had received by candle-light. He saw the difference at once and I had some anxious moments before he put his head down to feed. Next day, with the same amount of daylight, he began to feed without hesitation, so that next time I was encouraged to open the door another inch. After another couple of days he behaved well with quite an appreciable amount of daylight in the room. This was progress.

There has been no contretemps, no panic effort to escape, no ugly incident with which I could upbraid myself for lack of care. Quietly he is being led into his new life, and so far he has shown no dislike of its dawn. Soon he must emerge from his tunnel, from his hood, for longer intervals to enable him to see, and become accustomed to, more of the strange new world into which he is being taken. But before doing that it is necessary that he should gain some confidence in me, his travelling companion. He has lost his initial fear of me, but, naturally, much nervousness remains and I must get through that. If, while in the hooded state, he may still be regarded as travelling in a train through a succession of long tunnels, then it may be said that I must take my place in his railway compartment so that he can take full stock of me, and get to know me, before we reach the end of our journey. In one sense I have already sat opposite him, but so far he has been so occupied in having his food that he has not given me his full attention. I have raised the blind so that he can see outside, but as it is still only the half-light of early dawn he has not been able to see very far, no farther in actual fact than what the meagrely rationed daylight in the mews has allowed him.

My dominant desire is so to condition his nerves that he may wear the hood less. To effect that I must begin by getting inside the hood, in a manner of speaking, so that through our being together he may grow familiar with me. This is just another way of explaining the last paragraph. But his hood is too small for me to get inside it, so we must give him one large enough to take the two of us.

A small room, seven or eight feet square, like a cubicle but without a stick of furniture, an interior as bare and as plain as it is possible to be, will allow him but little more vision than what he has had within the hood, particularly as it will at first contain no more light than what he needs to see me by. It would be rather like putting a gigantic flower-pot over the two of us.

A keeper's cabin on wheels, the sort that is taken out to the pheasant-rearing fields, will provide what we want, and that I have. I do not take Genghis to it directly, for, having taken him off the perch in the mews, I take the first step towards teaching him to remain unmoved while the hood is put on him. Until now he has always been hooded up while preoccupied with feeding, in other words I prevented him, as much as I could, from giving the putting on of the hood his whole attention. To some degree he has become accustomed to the feel of its going on, but it has always been under cover of his feeding. The first time it was put on he refused to go on feeding, but every day since then he has continued to eat after it has been put on, which was exactly what I wanted, as it is necessary for him to receive the impression that my hooding him is of little consequence.

Now that I have taken him on to the fist I only half remove the hood by taking hold of its leather tag on top and pulling it forward, just so far as to uncover his eyes, then I push it back again without giving him a chance to look round. I repeat that a few times with a few minutes' interval in between. Yes, that is all right. His eyes are momentarily uncovered for as long as it takes him to think what now? At the first hint of apprehension in his eyes the hood goes back into position. He is now so accustomed to wearing it that he has come to associate its dark interior with security. It shuts out visions that cause him nervousness, so that it is almost a relief to him when it is put on again.

Forward to the keeper's cabin. Sacking has been put over its windows to exclude all but a little daylight. I take my stand and prepare to stay an hour or more in the dim interior. Off comes the hood, completely off this time. I hold it at the level of his crop, but while he is still dazed at the change of scene I put it on again. After this has been repeated a few times it becomes evident that the novelty of the scene is beginning to wear off. At first he gazed in amazement at the cabin's walls. Note that. I was but a secondary consideration, that much he has lost his fear of me. But the last time I unhooded him he looked directly at me, with an enquiring what-have-you-brought me-in-here-for look in his eye. I was waiting for that, and now that I have seen it I am bound to take it for the signal for beginning the next stage of the proceedings. So I hood him up, and for the first time he flinches just a little at the hood. He flinches at the hood because now that he fears me less he can give the hood more of his attention. Now that it is on I am filled with relief because that last time I saw just a bit of danger in his eyes, the danger that he might bate off the fist, but now that his eyes are covered again that danger has gone.

Eyes, eyes, eyes. A falcon in early training seems less a body than a pair of large, dark eyes that forbid the falconer to look squarely into them, not that he wants to because they glow with such an intensity that they almost burn him to look at them. Yet he must watch them, if obliquely, and in any case they are so commanding that he is conscious of them all the time.

The eyes of Genghis transcend his corporeality so that I feel that I am up against a spirit instead of a bird. When I am with him my body is pushed out because his eyes give it no recognition. It is his eyes against my eyes all the time. With the greatest respect I am trying to train him, but those eyes make me feel so abjectly separate. There never is, never was any question of 'doing battle' with a hawk in early training unless, by cruel chance, someone without knowledge of the subject takes on the job. At this stage I cannot convince Genghis that I am his friend, but I can, and must, show him by prudence that I am not his enemy, for as such I would never be able to fly him. Indeed sometimes I wonder whether I really have more power over him than he has over me, for if I am putting him under restriction it is also true that he is imposing self-restraint on me.

I unhood him again and there are his eyes looking at me so directly and steadily that for the first time I take a metaphorical step backwards, feeling just a little on the defensive. It is as if, for the first time, the subterfuge of dim interiors and new scenes is revealed to him, so that he stands in the full light of understanding, demanding of me an explanation for his present situation. His eyes neither challenge nor accuse but ask boldly, as a right, what it all means. The honesty in his searching look tells me that I am not regarded as an enemy. Wrested from his natural life in the Arctic he may be, but his growing tractability confirms that he bears me no hatred.

So we confront one another, as if weaponless, our relationship in suspense, but only for the moment because soon his attention begins to wander to the tiny world of no horizons in which he finds himself. His impulse is to fly away, to cross the incomprehensible frontiers and find again the only life he knows, the one that is within his experience, but he cannot see anywhere to fly to. Oppressed by vagueness he becomes restless, as the jerki of movements of his head indicate. He wants to break outng it all, to burst asunder the lying vision of entombment. 'You're nothing but a pack of cards!' exclaimed Lewis Carroll's Alice, and her appeal to reality delivered her from monstrous falsities. Perhaps, after all, this cabin is but a house of cards, an illusion from which the glorious reality of his wings will free him as it freed him from the enclosing mists of his native mountain.

The presentation of the hood must never precipitate a bate. It would only have to cause a few bates for harm to be done because the hawk, afterwards, would bate on sight of the hood and it would be difficult to break him of the habit. In other words he would become hood-shy, a condition as undesirable as it is unnecessary. Genghis was now about to bate from the fist; he was so keyed up for this action that the opportunity of checking the bate by hooding him was past. Very likely by an adroit and quick movement of the hand I could land the hood on his head, but that is not allowed because 'trick' hooding ends in hood-shyness. A hawk must be persuaded to *accept* the hood. There must be no deviation from this rule.

I can do nothing now to prevent his bating. He bates, and as I had hoped, did not hang from the fist by the few inches of jesses that he wears on his legs but was up again on the fist the same second as he felt their restriction. Now it is my turn for action, for if I were to continue to keep still he would bate again. I can only prevent another bate by diverting his attention, so smoothly and quietly I begin to pace the cabin before he has recovered from the surprise. He is so amazed at seeing the walls slowly going past him, as it appears, never before having perched unhooded on a moving object, that he keeps rooted to my fist. I find relief in my slow march. Before, my thoughts were piling up against the dam of my immobility, but now they are flowing smoothly again. Flowing smoothly, to Genghis, are the cabin's walls. What sort of a world is this where nothing is stable, where there is no horizon and no sky? He hardly looks at me, but always at those moving walls, and when I turn at the end of my few paces the whole of that little world revolves before him so that, more than ever, his feet grip the comparative security of my glove.

From his capture until now it was he who had the initiative and I could but humbly follow in the direction he decided to take, but now I no longer hang on to the elephant's tail because I am leading him by the head. I find it so stimulating to be ahead of him at last that my attitude to him becomes almost patronizing, and I begin to talk. He, of course, knows my voice very well now but at the moment he is too preoccupied to pay much attention to it.

Far from finding it tedious there is something quietly rewarding in this smooth pacing up and down. It is difficult to say whether it is a form of self-mesmerism. I only know that each time I turn at the end I feel that nothing in this life must prevent those few returning paces to the other end, and repetition persuades me that nothing can. I reach the end only to turn. I turn only to pace. It is continuity expressed in its simplest form.

For a long time, perhaps nearly an hour, he wonderingly tried to account for it all, for, even in the dream world in which he found himself, it was impossible for him to lose the habit of observing everything that went on around. Just put him on his pinnacle of rock where, on his native mountain, he used to wait for the wild duck to pass. There, nothing, absolutely nothing, would escape his keen vision. It was not that danger might take him unawares so much as his insistence that nothing should take place, nothing should happen, without his visual consent, for life must never get ahead of Genghis who lives over everything, the lord of the skies.

I continued to pace, up and down, up and down. Occasionally the jerking movements of his head indicated his contemplation of another bate, but each time I succeeded in persuading him to change his mind by raising him on my fist. The new position caused him to change the direction of his thoughts, for when close to the cabin's ceiling he had to look down, and always a hawk fears less when it is looking down than when it is looking up.

For a long time he watched those moving walls, trying to find an explanation. As long as he did that I was able to proceed with the next stage, but I knew that in the end he would give it up, and he did. He turned his head and looked at me appealingly—What does this mean? he asked with splendid boldness in his eyes. Thereafter he disregarded the moving walls as if they ceased to exist, and, instead, just kept his gaze on me. Every time I looked his way there were the two great eyes searching mine. So, in the last resort he was looking to me for guidance. In his changing world, in the shifting scenes, he was finding no stability, but he was realizing now that the one and only thing that did not change was myself, and his penetrating gaze showed very clearly that he was attracted by the thought that he might be able to trust me. For me this was not so much a triumph as the fulfilment of my expectations, but it was deeply satisfying to have him sitting perfectly still now on my fist while I walked up and down. He did not know, as I did, that he had now reached the most decisive moment of his life. He did not know, any more than I did, the exact moment when he decided to come with me. Far from being beaten he was standing at a new beginning, and now he was with me.

Within the close confines of the cabin's walls as I walk

up and down, talking to him, I feel that I can do anything with him because of his immobility and trustful gaze. So I take the hood and, while still pacing up and down, raise it up to his chin, as if going to hood him, and then lower it again. At intervals I repeat the motion. Raise, lower. Raise, lower. The object being to familiarize him with the preliminary movement of hooding. He remains completely unmoved. After ten minutes or so of this exercise I carry it a stage further by putting the hood up as far as his eyes and lowering it again. He does not mind at all while I repeat this for another ten minutes. After that I slip the hood on right over his head and in the same movement draw it off again. On and off. On and off. All the time walking and talking quietly to him. This is just naked hooding, no wrapping it up in the allurement of food. I want to get him so familiar with the act that, as time goes on, he will hardly give a thought to it. And now, every time I hood him I leave it on for a time, sometimes for a few seconds, sometimes for a few minutes. Sometimes I hood him midway, sometimes at the end of the cabin while turning. He takes it all with complete equanimity, never flinching an eyelid. Feeling pleased at this progress I keep repeating 'At last I've got you, I've got you!' as indeed I had. Before, when he was first hostile and then passive, he was little more than a bird that was kept quiet because it had a hood on, that could be carted around like a stuffed bird. Even in the later stages what little interest he had in me was balanced by a certain amount of distrust, but now he has come over to my side. His mentality has been directed into the right path. The next objective is to win his confidence. Never will he be violently converted. Only by continued kindness can his emergence from his former wild self be made complete, and of course it is always in his power to refuse further co-operation with me, if by any impulsive, hasty act or heavy-handed touch I offend him.

I bring my pacing to a smooth halt. The cessation of movement disturbs him as can be seen by the nervous movements of his head, but I have hooded him while moving, now I will hood him while standing still, and I do. That was all right. Off again with the hood, and on again before he begins to fidget nervously. A three-minute interval and I repeat. Well done Genghis! That's enough for today, and to my great pleasure he begins to feed immediately I place the raw meat over his feet. Certainly his spirit has suffered nothing from today's experience. I remove the hood so that he can feed bare-headed, and while he feeds I resume my gentle pacing. Always before he has fed while I sat motionless. Now my moving about adds yet another experience in the course of his training and he does not object. Before the meat is quite finished I hold the hood under his lower mandible. 'Come on Genghis, you know all about this now!' Smoothly, unhurriedly and without ruffling a feather, it goes on to his head and he finishes his feed, and O joy! for the first time he feaks on my glove, that is to say he rubs his beak on it to clean it, and then he rouses (gives all his feathers a shake), both of which are sure signs of contentment.

It was with a light step that I carried him back to the mews. Somehow he felt different on my fist, the difference between a newly caught hawk and one that was coming along nicely in its training. Two more days of these hooding lessons and now he stands perfectly to the hood, having no fear of it at all. Walking or standing it makes no difference. And during the hours that we have been closeted in the cabin he has got to know me a lot better. The cabin phase of his training is now over. He will never see that interior again for it has served its purpose. It is possible now to let more daylight into the mews, and by giving him tough wings of birds, with all the feathers on, to eat, his meal-time is prolonged so that I can keep him happily occupied on the fist for an hour and more while he deplumes his food and wrestles with pinion-joints.

In the evenings I take him into the house and, seated among visiting friends, with him on my fist, take his hood off every now and then to disclose, for a moment, his large wondering eyes. It is rather like taking photographs with him inasmuch as he receives an impression of the scene, but before over-exposure blurs the image on his mind in fright the hood is slipped back on his head again. By now he is well used to the sight of my old face but strangers' faces make him nervous as mine did at first, but he has to get used to them so I let him have these small glimpses to begin with. At each unhooding my face is within a few inches of his, and that, anyone would think, adds up to a little short of cruelty, especially as it is in full daylight, or electric light if the hour be late. Yet it does not even make him screw his eyes up or flutter them, so intent is he in taking in the sight of other people. This disregard of myself pleases me very much because it is just the same as if he were saying 'O him! I know he's all right!'

I have even unhooded him outside in full daylight but those exposures had to be of the briefest. Still, every day he is taking in new sights and receiving new impressions without any distress to himself, and the fact that that can be done through the judicious use of the hood is the measure of its value in training a hawk.

I have been allowing him more and more daylight in the mews for his feeds until every blind was raised. Only an outside screen cuts off his vision of the outside world. that wondrous sight still has to be denied him because he is hardly prepared for it yet. But it is coming to him.

Last night I unhooded Genghis on the perch for the first time. So far has he progressed that from now on he will not have to wear the hood at nights. Soon he will be wearing it very little during the day. I had to enter the mews with extreme care this morning. All light had been carefully excluded from its interior of course, so that he would sit quietly on the perch without fretting. As I opened the door a few inches the light streamed in and caught his eyes. He looked alarmingly alert. I kept speaking to him softly, wishing to enlist any possible aid to reassure him. Having squeezed myself in I closed the door behind me and waited for my eyes to become accustomed to the dark. Then I opened it half an inch so I could just see sufficiently to approach him. I had to move forward almost imperceptibly, wondering who was suffering the greater nervous strain, he or I. Only once before had I approached him when he had been unhooded and that was on his capture. He was terrified then, he was only nervous now, but nervous enough for his whole inclination to make him want to fly away from me. I did not approach him directly, but to one side, wanting him to attempt to move along the perch away from me. That he did, but being tethered by his leather jesses he could only move along about six inches. He began jumping against his jesses in an effort to free himself and under cover of his agitation and distracted attention I brought my gloved fist up underneath him so that it rested against his feet. It was garnished with the wing of a wood-pigeon. I had hoped that on seeing this he would seize it and begin to feed, but I had been a bit too optimistic for he still tried to get away from me. But it did not matter because next time he jumped I advanced my fist so that he landed on it. The moment he found himself on it the familiarity of his position made him change his mind. It took me but a few seconds to unleash him from the perch and then I did what any falconer would have done, raised him high up over the perch to forestall a possible bate. Once I was safely away from the perch I carefully lowered him, and before my fist was back to its usual position he had lost all interest in the proceedings having decided to turn his attention to the food. So that was all right. After he had eaten a few mouthfuls I hooded him and allowed him to continue picking the bone through the hood. It was not yet his feeding time but he could not get enough meat off the bone to give him anything like a meal, yet it served to keep him amused.

I carried him to the weathering enclosure where Robert, my falconer, had already put the peregrines on their wooden blocks to bathe and weather. The top of each block or wooden post is eighteen inches above ground level. A hawk is attached to the block by a leather leash, four or five feet long, and it spends its day sitting on the top of the post, preening itself, especially after a bath, or just enjoying the sunshine, or shade if it be hot, until its turn comes to be flown.

Trained hawks at my home would be in some danger if their weathering ground were not enclosed by a twelve-foot high wire-netting fence to keep out peacocks. These birds are most bellicose where hawks are concerned and if they had the opportunity would most certainly kill them. They have the advantage of size of course and very powerful legs, while a hawk is at a disadvantage when tethered. There is no doubt about it, peacocks do hate hawks and at least once in the past they have come near to doing mine an injury. I have known the tables turned but once and that, incredible as it may seem, was by a humble, mouse-eating kestrel! A wild one. I did not witness the scene but our gardener did, and as he is scrupulous in truthfulness I do not doubt his story. He had come in to his tea and was enjoying it in the window of his living-room which looks out into the walled vegetable garden. A peahen was walking about within his view, only fifteen or twenty yards away, when, without any warning, the kestrel flew on to her back and savagely attacked her. Our gardener says he did not see the kestrel's descent. The first thing he saw was the peahen's cutting wild capers in her effort to dislodge the little hawk. She succeeded in doing that but the kestrel, instead of flying away, stood his ground and raised his hackles at her. The peahen paid him out for his brazen effrontery by pecking and kicking him unconscious. Within the hour Bill had told me all about it. I took the kestrel, realizing that I held in my hands a unique example of the species, and would have wished intensely to guard his recovery, but unfortunately the damage done to him was beyond repair and he died that night. It was a young male.

Individual kestrels are, very occasionally, capable of the most surprising things. A young friend of mine took one from the nest and trained it. He called it Henry Blue-tail. Male kestrels do, of course, have blue tails, but after their first moult. This one, by some freak chance, grew his blue tail in the nest.

I think I am correct in saying that Henry showed no interest for flying small birds, as a merlin certainly would have done; in fact he disregarded everything that flew except his own kind. Whenever a wild kestrel appeared in the sky Henry used to fly out to attack it with the utmost fury and in doing so gave a fine exhibition in flying. To my knowledge he caught at least two, but he may have had more.

The first time I met Henry Blue-tail was when Terry brought him on a visit to Frog's Gutter, my hawking cottage in the middle of a grouse moor. He arrived at eleven o'clock in the morning and the first thing he did was to cast Henry off the fist. He flew round once and then headed for the horizon and was lost to sight.

'That's a funny way to fly a hawk, Terry; you'll never see him again!'

I had good reason for saying that because the country was entirely new to Henry, but Terry was not at all perturbed. He said there was no need to worry, Henry would be back by teatime.

We went out hawking in the afternoon, and had returned to the cottage where Terry went inside to put the kettle on while I was returning a hawk to its block in the weathering enclosure. I was about to enter the cottage when I heard the shrill *kee kee kee* of a kestrel overhead. I looked up and there was Henry sailing round in circles, high in the air. He had no use for me but he was calling for Terry, and continued to call for him until he emerged from the cottage. As soon as Henry saw him he closed up his wings and landed on Terry's fist as lightly as a zephyr. Goodness knows how many miles he had flown, but no doubt he had enjoyed himself and there he was back again, obviously as pleased to see Terry as Terry was to see him. And that was how Terry used to fly him every day!

To get a kestrel like that one is just a matter of luck. When I was young I tried my hand at training them and found them delightful pets. They used to fly very prettily but were no good for serious hawking. Wild ones are common up on the moor where I hawk, but although I have spent many hours watching them in flight I have never seen one fly at a bird. Sometimes they make mock attacks on my hawks but are always careful not to press the attacks too far. Even so one of them paid the penalty when a young falcon, that I was flying for the first time, suddenly turned on it and flew it in real earnest. A brilliant flight followed in which the kestrel flew to great heights in its attempt to throw off its pursuer, but my falcon, Aurora, stuck to her quarry grimly and finally killed it about three miles away.

On one occasion a wild kestrel showed extreme boldness, or foolhardiness, or perhaps it was just impudence. A friend and I had flown a falcon at a team of mallard. She had singled one out and after a good flight had killed it. She too was a young falcon and it was her first wild duck, so by way of reward and encouragement we left her to deplume and take her pleasure on it while we lit our pipes and sat in the heather and talked. When ten minutes had gone by I turned my head to look at the hawk and I shouted to my friend in amazement to take a look. There were two hawks on the kill and one was a little kestrel! Every moment I expected the peregrine to turn on the uninvited guest, but the little hawk looked quite ingenuous and the falcon did not seem to object to having it sharing her meal. Even so I thought the falcon's patience might wear out so, fearing for the kestrel, I got up and advanced on the two of them. I had reached within a few yards of them before the kestrel, with some show of reluctance, let go and flew away.

After entering the weathering enclosure I put a block in the early morning sunshine and put Genghis down to weather. An hour later I moved him and his block into deep shade, as these Arctic falcons soon become distressed under an English summer's sun.

A few days ago I had noticed that a peahen had chosen to nest under rhododendrons within fifty yards of the hawks' weathering enclosure. I felt uneasy about it as more than once the bird had been seen pacing up and down against the wire-netting, trying to get through to the hawks. Without realizing it the sight had been getting on my nerves, as she seemed so silently determined to wreck the harmony that prevailed on the other side of the netting. But from the day that this evil-minded bird first saw a gyrfalcon standing out head and shoulders, in every sense, above the peregrines she was driven to such fury that she more than doubled her efforts to break through the defences. In the main these were sound, but on the far side of the enclosure is an avenue of yews, which is valuable for providing the hawks with shade, and the intricacies of their branches are such that it was impossible to stretch wire-netting along their length, so we had to lace with ordinary strand wire instead, which was adequate for keeping unwanted livestock on the right side of the fence so long as they had the decency to be warned off by it. The peahen's nest being on the other side she had been content to try boring her way through the wire-netting without, of course, making any headway. But the gyr apparently held so much menace for the brood of peachicks she hoped to hatch and rear that she went the whole round of the defences to try and get at him, and more than once I saw her dangerously thrusting her front part through the strand wire to get at him where, under the yews, he was resting from the noonday heat.

I chased her off many times but always she returned. I could not remain there all the day and the family who lived in the cottage nearby, seeing this, most kindly posted guards when Robert the falconer was also unable to be there. It was hoped that by our sheer persistence, through our chivvying her about, she would give up, but she did not, nor was it possible to catch her until that moment of crisis when she finally burst through the wire to end all. Most fortunately, the man from the cottage was on the spot. She had barely got her whole body through when quick as lightning he shot an arm out and grabbed her by the tail. Soon afterwards she was safely tucked under my arm, and within a couple of minutes was safer still behind the locked door of a shed. Her eggs were collected and put under a hen.

A hawk can be said to be nearly half trained when that memorable day comes when it feeds outside in the open air, unhooded, on the fist. Genghis has done just that to-day. For three days previously I had fed him in the big barn, within reach of its open door. While he fed I walked about, every now and then allowing him just a glimpse of the outside world. Yesterday he had reached the stage when I could stand in the doorway, and to-day I had him right outside. When one considers that, all through the early days of manning and training, a hawk's every thought, every move, seems to indicate a passionate desire to get outside and fly away, it always seems strange when the time comes, however judiciously its training has been conducted, that it does not immediately attempt to escape. It was quiet outside but even so one would have expected the light evening breeze to make him restive with its whisper of freedom, but he looked less up at the sky than he did at me, and he did not look at me much because he was far more interested in his food. If that had been taken away from him at that moment he would have fought to free himself as if he had been only just caught. So delicate is the fabric of his present training that the least untoward incident would collapse the whole of it. Only time and continued judicious treatment can cement it. Had I thought of all this as I stood outside with him I might have become nervous, and if I had my nervousness would have been communicated to him. After all I had reason for nervousness for here was a bird that, such a short while ago, was 'as wild as a hawk', as free as air, superbly indifferent to man's interests and defied by nothing but the elements over which he was always superior. But here he was now at the very gates of freedom, never considering that he was tethered and never doubting that he could fly away at the moment of his choosing. He could not have thought me such a bad fellow because such had been his experience of me that he saw no reason now to show any preference for any other perch than my fist for the enjoyment of his meal.

It was tempting to let my thoughts range like this over the wastes of speculation, but the pressing need was to guard our growing intimacy. Such vigilance was called for that if, in absent-mindedness, I had let him swallow his last mouthful outside he would hardly have given me a look before bating in an attempt to fly away. That was why I had to steer him into the barn again, and before he had quite finished eating, with a roof over his head once more, I slipped the hood on and breathed a sigh of thankfulness that everything had gone so well. Back on the perch in the mews I unhooded him again for the night. I don't know what thought there was behind the look he gave me, but possibly it was not altogether unrelated to what I was thinking when I said to him, before closing the door:

'Well, we've got you outside at last, Genghis!'

For the next few days I continued to feed him outside, prolonging his meals until an hour was spent very pleasantly by both of us while in leisurely fashion he discussed his food. So much did our confidence in each other grow, that I was able to sit comfortably in a chair and enjoy the sight of this beautiful creature happily occupied under my care. But although I was thus able to relax my body there was still no question of being able to ease up in watchfulness. Everything had to be thought out even before taking him on to the fist. The chair itself had to be placed in exactly the right position where the evening sunshine could bathe him, where he could not be surprised by the approach of anything alive, and where, if by unhappy chance he should bate, his wing would not strike anything. On the right of the chair I placed a low table, so as to have spread out on it and available to my right hand joints of rabbit or of bird for his delectation. And where I put the chair I made sure that he would be able to see people, as they moved about, for it was part of his education that he should lose fear of a stranger's face. Occasionally I had to call out to someone to ask him to deflect his course a little if he was bearing down upon us. The sudden appearance of a dog or cat is the worst menace on these occasions, but fortunately neither of these was about because the whole place is a bird sanctuary, so consequently dogs and cats are not allowed in it.

I always had to be most careful in the closing stages of his meals, for it was still out of the question to have him unhooded on my fist, outside, without his being occupied in feeding in order to keep him from exploring any thought of trying to fly away. So it was necessary to judge just the right moment to raise myself out of the chair, very carefully to avoid frightening him, and to enter under cover of a building to hood him before he had quite finished eating. Nevertheless progress demanded that a day must come when I should have to hood him outside and, thank goodness, that passed uneventfully.

He is still rather nervous when I enter his mews in the

morning to take him out to the weathering enclosure. My approach to the perch still makes him uneasy and this must be expected because its significance is great. Man draws near to half-wild bird, and bird still cannot be quite sure that man's intention is an innocent one. The distance that separates us at that moment is the measure of that gulf that still lies between us. Good as his progress has been the gap has not yet been filled. My arm is stretched across it towards him during the day, but at nightfall I withdraw and we each retire into ourselves. It is this bridging of the distance between us next morning that is the worst moment of the day. If I were to cross without the flag of peace my approach would be more than he could bear. As it is he is inclined to take more note of me than of the flag, it is only when I wave the meat for his close inspection that he believes in me as the bearer of good-will. Once he is on my fist again his confidence returns.

Somebody once said that the training of a hawk is an art that would rejoice the heart of a psychologist. I rather doubt that but I do know that there is no better way for a man to get to know a bird, or the bird the man. If the hawk, in the process of training, is on trial for its intelligence and qualities of tractability and courage it is equally true that the falconer himself undergoes a most searching appraisement by the hawk in regard to his conduct and character. If the bird were to demand nothing short of perfection from the man no hawk would ever be trained, but if, in its generosity, it does not have to make too great allowance for human frailty hawk will like man. This training is a two-way business.

The number of hours Genghis had spent bare-headed on my fist outside must be considerable. His behaviour had been as good as possible. In this phase of his training he could not go any further and that indicated that he was ready for the next. The next step was to accustom him to sit, without the hood, on his wooden block in the weathering enclosure. This was part of the design to bring him more and more out of the hood. Great care was needed, however, because if this process was hurried forward prematurely too much of the wild Genghis would reappear and in the light his wild spirit would become strong again and cast out the growing tameness that I had been nurturing so assiduously.

So the day before this bold step forward was taken I fed him earlier than usual, and sparingly, in preparation, so that his sharpened appetite would be available to aid me on the evening of the following day when the great unhooding would take place. He had already, as related, spent some time, hooded, on the block, taking the air or 'weathering' as falconers call it, and he was doing just that when I unhooded him. The moment it was off he drew in all his feathers very tightly, in nervousness, when he saw where he was, and crossed his wings severely so that his flights stuck out like crossed swords. I had unhooded him in the evening, hoping that the failing light would excite him less than the bright light of day. Although I was within a couple of feet of him he gave me no more than a glance. I remained there, squatting on my heels, as still as a rock, while he stared in amazement at everything around. He was the picture of alertness and looked so horribly ready for the 'off' that I scarcely dared breathe. I wondered how long it could last. How long did it last? I do not know, perhaps five, perhaps ten minutes, and while I waited cramp began to steal into me and my body ached. Then he looked down at his feet and saw for the first time that he was standing on a block. Then he looked at me and I had to lower my eyes modestly under his gaze. I knew then what he was thinking. He mistrusted me in that position because he had never seen me in it before. It was almost a relief when he bated away from me, for under cover of his movement I was able to retire a few yards. His attention was diverted from me for the moment by the pull of the leash against him. When I looked up from my sitting position he was on the ground the length of the leash away from the block on the far side of course, leaning forward in his attempt to break the leash's restriction and trying to walk away at the same time. He was puzzled more than frightened at what held him back and for his lack of panic I gave thanks. Realizing that he was making no headway he turned and, seeing the block, thought he would be better off on its modest elevation, and, after only a little hesitation, flew on to it. I was pleased that he did not mind flying in my direction to regain it.

As I was by then sitting on the grass a little farther away from him he felt just a little easier this second time on the block, all the same it was obvious that he intended to spend no more than a minute or two on it while making up his mind to which part of the landscape he was going to fly. I could do nothing more than wait, for if I had approached then it would only have made him bate the sooner. As it happened he was soon off again and while his back was towards me I shuffled forward and stopped within six feet of his block. I hoped that my nearness would not put off his flying back on to it, but in this he disappointed me.

This first time out on the block, unhooded, is always revealing as to character. Genghis's reaction was about typical of the average. Occasionally the falconer gets a surprise as I did once when the subject was a wild-caught peregrine falcon, rather unpromising material one might think. That hawk appeared to enjoy being trained. The first time she was put on the block the first thing she did, on being unhooded, was to rouse and then stand on one leg, both actions being sure signs of contentment. While she was thus enjoying herself surveying the scene I slipped away for a piece of meat. While returning with it she caught a glimpse of it in my glove and immediately bated —towards me! She jumped to my glove like a flash as soon as I got within range. Delighted with her tameness I put her to a further test. I left the enclosure and returned in five minutes without meat, except for a couple of tit-bits in my pocket. On my reappearance she at once bated towards me, and on nearer approach she sprang to my fist, apparently not caring whether it held meat or not. There she stood, boldly looking into my face with the utmost friendliness in her eyes. I gave her the tit-bits which she took gently from my fingers and she showed some reluctance to leave the fist for the block. Thereafter that hawk always tried to get to me every time I entered the enclosure.

For a half-trained hawk her extreme tameness was of course unique, and the fact that Genghis did not behave like that did not discourage me one bit. While he continued to pull at the end of his leash I held out my gloved fist with meat on it. He hardly gave it a look, so while he was still making abortive efforts to break away from the leather leash's hold on him I wriggled my body over the grass towards him, freezing each time he looked back at me, and going forward at each of his renewed efforts to escape. Finally I manœuvred my glove so that it rested on the ground close to his feet. He turned his head towards it then remained still while contemplating the meat's attractions, but only for a few moments for then he caught hold of the meat with his beak and right foot. I let him feed like this until he had put his other foot on, then I gently raised my fist and held it aloft while untying his leash from the block. His confidence was at once restored now that he was feeding on the fist again. He fed contentedly for half an hour then I hooded him to carry him back into the mews, and there I unhooded him again for the night as soon as he was on his perch. The experience had done him good. The important thing was that he had not been frightened, and that his uneasiness had been ended as soon as he found himself back again on the familiar fist.

The next evening I put him out for about a quarter of an hour again. He was quick to recognize the block and spent more time on it than on the ground. He very nearly allowed me to take him up off the block to a piece of meat on the fist, but funked it at the last second and bated. I drew back a little to let him regain the block, which he lost no time in doing, and on my second attempt to take him up he stepped on to my fist and immediately began to feed.

By the fourth day he was beginning to look nearly as composed in the weathering enclosure as his neighbours the two peregrines, and that was the day when he first jumped from the block to the fist. For the latter I was especially thankful because it ended a small period of anxiety. It is always rather unpleasant and nerve-racking having to approach a hawk that looks as if it is trying to make up its mind to fly away from you, and I am glad to say I no longer had this discomfort in taking Genghis off the perch in the mews first thing in the morning. Thus at no turn during the course of the day did he now show fear of me. He was altogether coming along with me because nothing further remained in our personal relationship to disconcert him.

For the first few days he was permitted to remain unhooded on his block for short periods only because the process of acclimatization must be regulated so as to aid the outgoing of his old life and the incoming of the new. To take him along too fast, by over-exposing him to conditions that hitherto have been so utterly outside his experience, would be like putting the pressure on the wrong end. It would reverse the current of his progress so that his old wildness would flow back into him. If he were left unhooded outside all the day long in the early stages he would suffer too much from the impression that he is tied up and that would call his wildness back. But by gradually lengthening these periods he was getting the measure of his leash. His neighbours the peregrines, old in training, have theirs taped to a nicety, so that when they jump off their blocks they receive no violent jerk at the end of the leash.

By the end of a week he was allowed outside, unhooded, for a couple of hours and he showed every sign of enjoyment, preening, rousing, and standing on one leg. Occasionally he would jump down to the ground, turn, and in one great bound would plant himself squarely on the block again. During these hours outside he was never left alone. If I could not stay with him, my falconer, whom by now he knew quite well, would have to be there. It would have been dangerous to have left him unattended for then he would have found himself without human company and we could not at that time afford to run the risk of his discovering that our absence was more of a relief to him than something to be desired. I had been doing all I could to prevent his getting such an impression by giving him tit-bits at the block every now and then. Apart from that I used to walk about the enclosure much of the time so as to turn his attention inwards as a means of preventing his gaze and his thoughts being beguiled by the allurement of distance. I knew too well that the distant scene would entice his roving thoughts and make his wings itch for action at the recall of wide open spaces. As another way of checking this tendency I gave him tiring, which is the falconer's word for bones and sinews with but little meat on them; these he had on the block, and they had the desired effect of keeping him happily occupied for many hours while he pulled and tugged at them. The exercise they gave him was not only beneficial to his health, it also absorbed some of his pent-up energy.

The progress of a hawk at this stage of its training in particular is a fascinating study. It is a big responsibility too because it is so easy for everything to go the wrong way. The falconer must be constantly on the tips of his toes in watchfulness. He must never be a second behind but always a minute in front so as to anticipate any undesirable move on the part of his hawk, and always he must guide to keep it on the straight and narrow path that leads to progress. Another lesson that Genghis had to learn from my walking about inside the enclosure was to get used to man's approach. He had already succeeded in this by means of my giving him tit-bits. After that he had to become accustomed to my walking up to him without his having that reward. Whenever he looked like bating on a near approach I would forestall it by changing direction, and then I would continue to walk round and round him, gradually circling closer and closer round his block as and when he allowed it. He did not like my passing behind him too closely, but his repeated turning round to face me was useful in that it kept his attention from wandering outwards. He was really very good because, in addition to an inherently generous character, he was artful enough not to forget that I was liable to slip him a tit-bit occasionally, and that kept him friendly-disposed to me. It was amusing to see his look of disappointment when I would brush right past his block without giving him one, and when I did give him one to see his look of regret when I passed on because I did not stay to give him another.

Robert took turns at walking round him and so did a falconer friend who was staying with me. Their doing so was part of the plan to get him accustomed to mankind generally. But as I was his trainer the other two men did not offer him tit-bits on the principle that if he would suffer their approach without them he would regard mine gladly. Experience has taught me that it is not wise to have a hawk equally as friendly with every man as it is with its trainer. Every man means every stranger too and strangers cannot always be relied upon to treat a trained hawk with the respect that it deserves. More than once in the past my hawks have got themselves into trouble because they erred in the belief that every man was their friend.

As the days went by it was possible to leave Genghis outside on his block for longer periods until, in the end, he was left out, unhooded, all the day. By then he would take a bath, in the little concrete pond in the enclosure, and for the next hour would enjoy himself drying and preening in the sun until he was dry when I would move his block into the shade.

He has become so tame that it is no longer necessary for someone to be with him all the time while he is outside. My entry into the enclosure is an event that he looks forward to. As soon as he catches sight of me in the distance he spreads his wings and fans them in pleasurable anticipation, and as soon as I get anywhere near him his eagerness nearly always gets the better of him so that he bates towards me in his efforts to get to me. Now he springs to the fist from the block with an impatience that takes no account of whether he is likely to receive a tit-bit. In the mews he no longer holds back on the perch when I go in the morning to take him outside. The very first sight of him reveals that the sound of my approaching footsteps filled him with pleasure. He steps on to the fist with an eagerness that is delightful to see. After hooding him I still reward him with a tit-bit or a piece of tiring on the fist, but in another two or three weeks these sops will have become unnecessary, nor will it be necessary to hood him for the short journeys between the mews and the weathering enclosure.

Now that his home life under man's protection has become firmly established, the exciting stage has been reached when we can prepare him for the air. As so much concentration has been required to get him to his present position it might be asked how much more will be needed before he can be trusted to fly entirely free, if there is to be any prospect at all of his returning of his own free will to man, his captor. If he persists in regarding me as his captor then there would indeed be little chance of getting him back after his first flight however benevolently he, the prisoner, may have been treated. But the fortunate fact is that so many new impressions have since crowded his mind that his very earliest one, that of being captured, has been pushed out long ago. Even so if, during the course of his training, or even at the time of capture, there has been any single moment of wilful ill-treatment you can be sure that he will not forget that, for a malicious act is indelibly stamped on a hawk's mind. It would never be forgiven. Anyway, any suspicion against me of ill-treatment can be disproved by his present amiable behaviour and increasing confidence in me. Until now the main task has been to prove to him that I am his friend. Now that he has accepted that he and I can go forward together, and the work that still remains to be done will be as a holiday compared with that which has gone before. In another week or ten days, at the most, it will be possible to remove his leash and the swivel that connects the leash to his jesses, and to let him fly off the fist in fair confidence that it will be his free choice to return to me out of the air. There will be no guarantee that he will not chase a distant bird and perhaps kill it miles away and so get lost, but then his failure to return to me would be a matter of chance more than his choice. His early flights will be an operational risk with his goodwill towards me weighing in my favour. As time goes on he will become familiar with the country over which he is to be flown, so that the risk of his not returning to me after a long flight will become reduced because he will know better where to look for me.

This business of transforming a wild bird into a tame one, so that on liberation it will prefer to fly back to its captor instead of flying away from him, may seem too idealistic to be true. I should indeed be guilty of misleading you if I were to give the impression that a trained hawk is governed entirely by sentiment. The prosaic truth is that, after a flight, the hawk returns to the falconer because it has good reason to expect that he will provide it with a meal. The trained hawk, no less than the wild one, hunts only when it is hungry, so that the falconer flies it only when its meal time approaches. That is no more than the barest statement of the facts which, unless amplified, would also mislead the reader. There are other aspects of the matter that have to be considered, for instance the hawk might prefer to give up any intention of returning to the falconer, preferring to hunt for itself until, sooner or later, it kills. That is a course that it certainly would follow if its experience of the falconer be such that it would rather go its own independent way than trust to any co-operation with him. Whether it would or not hinges entirely on that word 'trust'. In other words the hawk must have confidence in its trainer and the trainer can win that confidence no less by unfailing kindness than by his skill in the art of training. The wonder is that any kind of understanding between man and a creature as wild as a hawk can be established at all.

By now Genghis has learnt to rely upon me as the provider of his food, but he has yet to learn to fly to me for it. If I were to put him on the wing to-day I should have no means of recalling him. He might circle round me once or twice and I could hold up a juicy piece of meat for him and he might return to the fist for it. But more likely the flying would go to his head and his enjoyment of it would temporarily put out of his mind all thought of food. The only course open is to begin by inducing him to fly short distances to me for his meal so that he will possess it before realizing that he is free. Actually he will not be free for the first few days because I shall tie a light line to the swivel in his jesses to prevent any possibility of an accident, though it will be unlikely that he will know that it is on him. Instead of inducing him to fly to the fist I shall tie his food to an object that falconers call the lure. Basically the lure is a wooden disk, seven or eight inches in diameter. It is weighted on one side so that, when thrown, it will always fall right side uppermost. It is wrapped with red felt, and sewn up, to enable a hawk to grip it in its talons, and the red is to make it conspicuous. On the one side strings are attached for the tying on of meat. That is the lure. To it is attached five or six feet of cord so that it can be swung about in the air.

Once a hawk understands the significance of the lure, that its appearance means food, it finds it more attractive to fly to than to the fist. To hold one's fist out at arm's length does less to advertise the meat it holds than does a lure, with meat tied to it, when it is swung in the air. A swung lure not only arrests a distant hawk's eyesight effectively but identifies the man who swings it as the falconer.

But in teaching Genghis the lure for the first two days it will simply be placed on the ground by his block. Despite the meat on it its unfamiliarity will make him hesitate over jumping down to it, but on the second day he will come to it well enough. On the third day he will come five or six feet to it, on the fourth three or four yards, on the fifth seven or eight yards, and so on until the ninth day when he will fly forty-five yards over a straight course to the lure. On the tenth day, with no string attached, he will fly entirely free for fifty yards.

For the last few days of this straight flying to the lure he will be taken up to the moor over which he is to be flown at grouse, so that the terrain up there will not be entirely new to him when he finds himself up in the air, high over it, entirely free. But before he goes up there he must undergo the little ceremony of having bells put on him, one on each leg. The occasion marks his readiness for flight. They are very special bells that come all the way from Pakistan. They have been copied in Europe but the brass from which the imitations are made is not of the right kind and they are not so resonant as hawk bells from the East. The latter are so good that, although no larger than a grape, they can be heard nearly half a mile away on a still day.

The purpose of the bells is twofold. To advertise that the hawk wearing them is not a wild one so that it will not be shot, and to enable the falconer to establish the bird's whereabouts by ear should it kill some distance away in deep heather, bracken or any other cover.

CHAPTER V

The very word falconry smacks of medieval romance, of chivalry, of knights and castles and baronial banqueting halls. Royalty practised it and discussed its finer points with courtiers who would have felt boorish without intimate knowledge of the art. Exiled princes and princesses pursued the sport in the demesnes of the great houses. The falcon was a symbol, the burnished, steely hard bird of the nobility. In the minds of men it took its stand on the summit of the ivory tower of aspiration. It lured the imagination into the realms of fantasy where young manhood put on the armour of virtue to venture through deserts of self-discipline in quest of a fabulous blue falcon or a white falcon of surpassing excellence, symbols of the unattainable that haunt the dreams of men.

Such imagery was translated into the search for more courageous and braver falcons, birds that would fly faster and higher at swifter, stronger and more elusive quarry. The noble peregrine was justly esteemed as man's faithful ally in the chase, and right well did she acquit herself then as she does now. But always falconers looked farther and farther away for better and better hawks, believing that the farther they went and the greater the hardships they endured the more would Providence reward their endeavour. They penetrated the mysteries of the East. They fitted out ships and sailed away on special hawk-catching expeditions to lands within the arctic circle where they found the great gyrfalcons that can outfly the gales that rage up there, magnificent predators that nature has endowed with the strength and the fortitude to rise superior over the boreal blasts and the blizzards.

Larger, faster and more powerful than the peregrine, the beautiful hierofalco, the gyrfalcon, is at the pole of perfection, but, as if it were not enough that they be difficult to procure, man not only had to master the art of training them, he had also to learn how to preserve their health which is attuned to life in cold latitudes. Neither of these tasks was easy, but falconers of the Middle Ages had much more success than their successors of the present day.

The training of Genghis had been an experience that had affected my habits of thinking and my pattern of daily life more than any other hawk that I had taken in hand. With the peregrine, the merlin, the goshawk and the sparrow-hawk modern falconers have a knowledge of training that comes directly from the past, but how to train a gyr and maintain it in health is largely a lost art. Therefore I was anxious about Genghis and the state of tension he kept me in made me feel that I was indeed embarked on an adventure.

On this same moor where I am now standing my friends and I have had good sport in the flying of our peregrines at grouse and wild duck. But in the season that has already opened I have taken it on myself to prove that the gyrfalcon still remains the master performer. So far I have said nothing of this secret hope to anyone, for to talk about it would, I feel, be sure to attract disappointment because any form of boasting usually has its dire reward. '*Je ne dis rien,*' says my French friend as he goes forth with falcon on fist, well knowing that the time to do the talking is when, having flown her, he brings her safely back again. In like manner, after a becoming spell of silence, another friend casts his handsome Saker falcon into the air with a terse '*Bismillahi!*'

So then! In the names of Odin, Wotan, Thor and all the Nordic gods away you go! and Genghis is free again, flying up and up towards the sun.

The blinding dazzle makes me shield my eyes. There is little I can see of him, hardly the rapid beating of his wings, but my heart beats as wildly as he climbs steeply into the boundless blue, and the only answer my eyes can get is the blinking, winking of rippled sunlight from the illumined edges of his wings as his body thrusts through the immense calm of the morning air. Before I let this wild thing off its chain I did not know what it was going to do except that it would fly, and now it appears to have chosen the golden path to the sun.

I have remarked how the training of a hawk affects the whole tenor of a man's daily life. In a sense part of his life has been invested in that of his hawk so that she becomes a creature of his own making in so far as she has been wrested from the wilds and fashioned anew to develop his unborn aspirations. It is a time of vigil for the falconer lest through any failing on his part there come a conflict of loyalties in his hawk when her confidence in him may recede and a hankering flare up for her former independent way of life.

When a man casts his hawk into the air she bears upward a part of him, something that is shared only between him and her, so indefinable that it would be impossible for him to reveal it to others either through conversation or any other medium, and he would be hard put to it to explain it to himself. So, with his hawk in the air above, he takes up a position in which he becomes exposed to the hopes and the fears of his own creating because of her.

With my hawk in the air above I wondered to what extent, if at all, our reciprocal relationship was disturbed. At the moment, being on a higher physical plane, he must look down on me if he wants to see me at all, and that just about reflects his habitual mental attitude to me, for when a hawk gives the falconer its attention one gets the impression that it is showing condescension to an inferior, and that, of the two, the falconer is the junior partner.

I had stared up at Genghis long enough for my aching eyes to become blurred with the strain. Subconsciously I reflected that if sight lost him in outer space my claim on him, too, would disappear. A gyrfalcon was being flown for which there was but very little known precedent to go by. Suddenly he emerged from his vehement ascent and, on set wings, cut across the considerable distance in my direction, letting it be known that he had not forgotten me. He drove right on without hesitation or the making of any adjustment, and in unbroken rhythm swung round in a half-circle salute over my head with such grace in the clean blades of his outstretched wings that my pride rose to meet him and became magnified in the thought of how very well spent had been the hours of his training. What I had put into them resulted now in his staying up over me when he could just as easily have been over the next county in the same time.

To take up a position whereby I was connected with the mystery of flight, in a bird that exhibited it to such perfection, was in every sense an uplifting experience. Not only was there my own vested interest in it but, what was much more moving, there was the beauty of the spectacle of a noble falcon of the Arctic behaving in a way so complimentary to me. Looking up I saw the pale undersides of his great wings that were edged with silver against the blue sky. The suddenness of the spectacle held me as when a visionary ship with immaculate sail excites the imagination. A ship! A ship! that sails as a conqueror! my thoughts sang even as the little silver trumpets shrilled in the rigging.

In the immensity of the sky there may have been other birds flying but he was the only one that flew for me. Underneath it all stretched the moor, centuries ago a royal forest. Far below him a herd of wild ponies raced over it, kicking out at each other in play and making the pollen of the heather fly in purple mist. They galloped and the thudding of their hooves increased its tempo as they passed me in a spurt of speed. When they had gone only their distant laughing whinnies reached my ears. I heard nothing else except the faint tinkling bells on the feet of the hawk that circled high above. I had heard bells before, against this same background, when a long white line of pierrots had appeared in the distance. Their line of advance was ragged with the indiscipline of fun as they quick-marched out of step to uproarious jazz. An evil subtlety underlay their jocularity and their exaggerated high-stepping raised clouds of dust out of the heather which was all dead in my dream. Their conventional, billowing white dress was studded with black pom-poms, and on top of each nodding conical white hat a hawk's bell jingled. What semblance of formation they had broke down completely as they bore down on me. Singing their ragtimes discordantly they elbowed me roughly as they strutted by and I fell in the dust. When they had gone I stood up and found that my wallet, containing all the money I had, was gone. Afterwards someone else came and I told him what had happened. I put my hand into my inner pocket to prove the loss of the wallet but found it was there after all, and in the same moment I saw that the heather was green again.

Far away some people were running. Like little dots they moved over the heather as if urged on by excitement. First the ponies and now the people. Up there on the moor that lovely morning it seemed that anything alive had to come my way, for it became evident that those four people, two adults and two children, were heading in my direction. They slowed down when they arrived at the bottom of the long slope, on the summit of which I was standing, but with the eagerness of childhood the two little ones started running again as soon as I was able to recognize them—they were the two children from the cottage, Harriet and Emma. Harriet soon outdistanced Emma, being the elder by six years, and I did not have to wait long for her arrival. She was out of breath and nearly speechless, but not quite, after her exertions, and her eyes shone in the red of her heated face as she laughed and pointed upwards. For her Genghis was free, and she had come to share both the falconer's and the hawk's rejoicing, not to ask questions as to how he was to be persuaded to return.

I now had but one desire, to get that hawk down before the others arrived, for he had begun to drift away when he saw that two people were below him instead of one. Hurriedly I explained the situation to Harriet, and she, good girl, did not stop to chatter but turned and ran down the hill to warn off her sister and father and mother.

I put my hand into the bag that hung on my back and pulled out the lure. As I swung it I put the referee's whistle to my lips and blew with such anguish that I felt I was calling him back from the other side of eternity. I was caught between two worlds, the avian and the human, for both were watching me, the hawk in silence, not so the human party for the two children were shouting for joy.

From high above and far away, Genghis, in obedience to my signal, shot forward and dived earthwards. His onrushing form was no longer that of a winged creature for the swiftness of his descent forced him to close his wings so that he became a solid bullet. For me it was a moment of exaltation because he was returning to me in as direct a line as possible instead of flying away. With my feet planted heavily on the ground I yet felt as light as my hawk for at that moment I was no less alive than he. 'He's your hawk,' I told myself for just then I was reaping joy, as he was, after weeks of intensive training. Had he nursed any lingering dislike of me he would not have been so anxious to annihilate the distance that separated us, for it seemed that his mental image of me was undimmed by distrust and unclouded like the clean air that he clove in naked speed. A screaming whistle passed over my head as the air rushed through his bells, and then he turned to come in. In my excitement I scarcely saw his alighting on the lure by my feet.

In his life there have been two hawks. First it was Genghis the wild, now it is Genghis the tamed. Likewise my mind, too, is divided in regard to him. First there was the leading of the captive through the labyrinth of training, now there is the joy of flying a free bird in the open sky.

From the lure he sprang to my fist. He looked lovely with the freshly painted look of a clean-run salmon just out of the sea. While he was feeding I looked down and saw that the warmth of the growing day had drawn the chill mists out of the surrounding lowlands, as it often does at this time of the year. They lay white over the plain so that distant hills looked like islands in a sea. The mists filled the nearby valleys and when they halted from their upward march. Harriet and Emma and their mother and father were no longer in sight. Genghis and I were alone in our mutual pleasure.

If the training of a hawk affect the tenor of a man's day-to-day life it is his subconscious mind chiefly that is stirred. Later, when the basic training is finished and the hawk is being flown, man's pleasure comes to the surface, for the main responsibility is passed to the bird, and the better it becomes the more does its human partner take on the role of spectator. But, like all other creatures led into the service of man, hawks vary greatly in regard to efficiency, and the really good ones are in a small minority. King Ethelbert wrote to Archbishop Boniface '. . . I wish you to procure me one thing besides . . . two falcons of such skill and courage as readily to fly at and seize cranes and bring them to the ground. The reason why we ask you to get such birds and send them to us is, of course, that very few hawks are found in our part of the world, that is in Kent, which produce eyasses that are much good: and it is quick-witted and high-spirited birds that are required for manning and training for the aforesaid art.' Modern falconers can appreciate exactly how he felt for it seems that the best hawks are always the most difficult to obtain. It has been written that no gyrfalcon ever flies badly and certainly Genghis is no exception. In flight he is more powerful, has greater speed and stoops harder than any peregrine. In him I have a treasure beyond price. I suspected it all along his training, but now that he has proved himself the knowledge of it is so thrilling that I do not doubt my very pulse is quickened. I suppose I feel rather like an artist who has been secretly at work on a masterpiece and who can now stand back while the world admires it, except that the picture is entirely the man's creation and the falcon is basically God's. I have done no more than claim my dominion over the fowls of the air, a gift that is in all of us if the Bible is to be believed, although, where falconry is concerned, far more use was made of this gift in the Middle Ages than is now made in the present century.

Now that I can take Genghis out of the mews, at the beginning of the day, and put him on his block outside in the knowledge that in an hour or two he will be flown entirely free, life feels even better than it did before, if that be possible in an existence where 'I've got the sun in the morning and the moon at night' with all its implications as numerous and as splendid as all the stars of the firmament too. To be in partnership with a bird that one can send up into the clouds and that will willingly return to one's feet on being recalled seems to me to be getting back to something fundamental, something for which we are the poorer when it is lost through civilization's drift from the world of nature. The late Revd. Gage Freeman, a celebrated falconer, who was 'Peregrine' of the *Field*, wrote 'Not to speak it profanely I declare that to see a trained hawk come out of heaven, frequently with the zigzag of lightning, upon rapidly flying grouse, sends a something through my whole frame, so thrilling in its pleasure, that I almost fancy, in some previous state of existence, I must have been the real peregrine himself.' And again, 'There is no flinching with the falcon . . . but there is downright, headlong, rapid, earnest, brave, honest, mighty chashing—there is the very character of commanding power in every hiss of her rushing bell, and in every stroke of her glorious wings. . . . Surely she is the queen of the wilderness and of the sky, the ruler of every creature beneath, the servant of but one above her! It is she to whom the winds are nothing, the hail nothing, the lightning on the mountains nothing—all these she defies; but man is her master, and I have seen her go out furiously at his bidding, or come down gently to his feet, out of the very clouds of heaven.'

In all things Genghis appears to reflect the contentment in my mind. On the perch in the mews he receives me with a welcoming chuckle and he bows and puts his head close to mine. Outside, on the way to the weathering enclosure, the sudden greeting of the sunshine makes him open his wings and dance on the fist. He looks into my face to invite my sharing his mood, and when I waggle my head at him he turns his upside down as if to out-do my clowning. He is quick to respond when I want to play the fool. On entering the weathering enclosure I have to shield with my body his view of the block until we are in leash-range of it when he flies to it with gusto. I drop the glove on to the ground and he springs on to it and plays with it like a kitten while the end of the leash is being tied to his block. Then I throw a rubber ball to him and he springs into the air to catch it before it falls to the ground. I make pretence of wresting it from him while he equally pretends to resist all my efforts. In play and at any other time he never, never bites nor claws me, for in all his character there is no corner of treachery. His five-foot leash gives us a diameter of ten feet in which to play ball. I throw it and he makes a flying leap after it to retrieve it to my feet, and in his eye can be seen the sparkle of amusement while he waits for me to throw it again. Fortunately the cottage family, Robert and a falconer friend, people whom he knows, have witnessed this fun, otherwise it would not be believed. I have never had a peregrine that would let itself go like this for they are too conscious of their dignity. Even he will not play when a stranger is watching. Instead he never takes his eye off the stranger but watches him every second of the time as if deeply intent on reading his character.

Except on his journeys to and from the moor, and previous to flying, he no longer wears the hood, but when the occasion demands his wearing it he accepts it without protest. In fact to see it go on him one would say that he likes it, as he never turns his head away from it.

After breakfast, when the sun is beginning to get hot, I revisit him to offer him a bath which he takes, with obvious enjoyment, about twice a week. Before he begins to feel the heat of an English summer's day I move his block into deep shade. On my approach he bates towards me jumping about in his excitement, at the end of the leash, as a dog would. Having shifted him to the shady part of the lawn he is often loath for me to leave him, seizing the end of my trousers with his talons and hanging on to it.

When the hour arrives to fly him how eagerly he springs to the gloved fist! for he knows very well what is coming to him. On release he climbs steeply up, up and up, high into the sky, and his bells ringing so gaily put to music his own soaring spirit. And then I walk the moor with him for escort circling above me, sometimes a mere dot in the heavens. Sometimes he has had enough of flying before I have finished my walk, and then, without waiting for me to produce the lure, he folds his wings and rushes through the air in a breath-taking descent, to alight on the ground by my feet, and then he looks up at me, demanding my fist for perch.

Soon Genghis will be ready for flying at grouse over the moor. It will be holiday time and I shall take him to a little cottage known as Frogs' Gutter, in the middle of the moor. There my falconer friends and I shall live for a time, but no gun-fire will be heard for we hunt only with our hawks.

CHAPTER VI

Harriet and Emma were at play. I stood to watch them in concealment. They played on the lawn against the bulge of the big rhododendron. It was no running-about kind of game but a quiet, almost contemplative one that required their close attention to little objects that they moved and pushed about on the turf. Every now and then the elder child called something that I was not close enough to hear, and this was repeated less precisely by Emma who always seemed a little late in her turn. Harriet's whole attitude was of the sweet condescension that only a child can show to a younger one. A pretty patronage that gave her more entertainment than the game itself for indeed she was a bit old for it.

As for myself I had just come off the moor where I had been flying Genghis. Until now all his flights had been training ones in preparation for his flying at grouse. Had he been a young peregrine he would have been ready for grouse on the opening day of the season, August the twelfth, but being a gyr I had to proceed with greater caution. He had felt the heat and consequently I dared not take the risk of letting him exert himself too much in the pursuit of grouse, but the hot days of summer had passed into the invigorating, cool ones of autumn and I had decided that this morning's would be his last training flight.

And now there I was, on the drive's verge, watching the children. They had created for themselves a little world of the moment that I was loath to disturb, for in it was a completeness, a quiet happiness that was independent of the whole state of earthly existence. I was sadly disquiet at being so hopelessly outside of it.

One feels so heavy, large and coarse when intruding on children's occupations that the wonder is that they do not shrink away as they would on the approach of a bear. The fact that they do not should make us thankful that earthly experience has not obliterated the fundamental simplicity which they see in us, even if our contemporaries do not. It seems incredible that there can be a friendship between a little girl and a middle-aged man but it happens, and when it does she is not interested at all in his worldly achievements, or lack of them. What matters to her is the way he feeds her imagination and the little secret world that is established between them. It is a delightful relationship because in it one is freed from the personal comparisons that always exist between adults. And age does not count. Emma is not conscious of hers, except in those moments when she sees it simply as a figure, and my own is so far outside her comprehension that whether it is thirty or sixty makes but little difference. It may be said with some truth that however a man may appear to the world a child sees him as he really is.

There is an irresistible fascination in the building up of a separate little world in which man and child are the creators. In it he leads her by the hand while she demands of him constant revelation. Last spring I invented a mischievous fairy for Emma's entertainment. The excuse for its introduction came when she pointed out to me one morning how certain of her toys that she had left out in the garden had been disarranged. Of course he had been kicking them around. Hadn't she ever caught a glimpse of him? Well, I had. That very morning as I was on my way to put the hawks out he ran across the lawn and I chased him and caught him before he could escape into the shrubbery. He was dressed in green and wore a little peaked hat. In my hand he squeaked with rage and fright and wriggled so much that he slipped through my fingers and all that I kept of him was a bit of his beard. (Later I produced a pinch of sheep's wool which entirely convinced her.)

'Emma,' I said. 'When you catch him clutch him tightly and don't let him go. Now show me how you are going to hold him.'

'Like this!' she said with determination.

'No, that's no good—he'll slip out here!' and I pushed my finger into her outstretched, podgy little fist.

'Like this?'

'That's better!'

I went on to tell her how he gets up into trees sometimes and that on a windy day he might get blown into her hair, so she must keep it well brushed otherwise he will get entangled in it. She listened attentively to all I had to say about him until she was red in the face with excitement. Then she caught my hand and asked me not to tell anyone about this fairy, inwardly fearing that her sister would kill it with scorn. But one day her mother overheard something of our secret for I was to discover that she had added the incident to her statistics that established my being a complete fool. Nevertheless I continued to put reality into the little man. In my repeated attempts to capture him there were times when I tore off a bit of his clothing. Once I put a tiny, pointed shoe into Emma's hand as proof that it had been a near go that time. When, one early morning, I surprised him *flagrante delicto* muddling up her toys I really did hang on to him at last, but finally put him down and let him run up the bank and into the hedge after he had promised to make restitution for his mischief making. So after an interval for preparation I told Emma of my success, and when she wanted to know what he was doing to put things right I said that he had left a message for her, a message that I could not understand but perhaps she could, the little man had gabbled it, and all that I had got from him was something about a box by the gate, a box and chocs. I appealed to her for help in solving the mystery, for, said I, there is no box by the gate. 'Yes there *is*,' she shouted, and, red in the face, she ran off to put her hand into the box that I had seen her father nail to the gate-post, the day before, for the postman's convenience. Naturally, Emma proved that the fairy had promised truly, but not until that moment did I learn that the chocolate manufacturers, whose familiar name adorned the wrapper in golden letters, were purveyors to the fairies. Clutching the chocolate she ran past me into the cottage, so I cleared off, not wishing to be confronted by her mother before whom I feel embarrassed when caught putting on an act.

This idea of the fairy's making restitution led me on to thinking of something else. I secretly bought a quantity of brightly coloured rubber balls. One day while Emma was playing on the lawn I pitched one at her from the terrace above, keeping myself hidden. When later she showed it to me it was for me to express amazement and mystification because, being only a little child, her reaction was nothing more than inarticulate bewilderment. When I told her that, beyond any doubt, it was a present from the fairy who was now sorry for having mixed up her toys, she accepted the explanation as if there could be no other. From that day onwards I seized every opportunity of throwing more balls. Plop! they fell near her and then I would run up the other side of the yew hedge and escape into the walled garden. She soon learnt the general direction whence the balls came so I had to be increasingly careful to avoid being spotted on throwing them. In time quantities of them starred the living green of the lawn with their garish colours and I had to stop, because her mother and father made it plain that they regarded them as an infestation. Far more pleasing to the eye just then were ever-present pairs of goldfinches. Throughout the rest of the year we lose them in the fields and open spaces but in the springtime the blossom draws them in and they bring enchantment to the garden. Their happy music tinkles through the apple trees and when they emerge from the banks of blossom to wink their pretty colours Matthew calls the children out to look at them. Really, what need is there to invent fairies when there are such as these about?

After this digression I would remind you that I am still concealing myself from Harriet and Emma who are at play by the big rhododendron. The door of the cottage opens to reveal their mother who is sniffing the air for any mischief her children might be brewing. She never misses a thing and very quickly sees me.

'Hello!' she says, 'you're back early this morning.'

'Yes. . . . Rather a nasty thing happened. . . . I've lost Genghis.'

Her eyes opened so wide and horror so transformed her face that the stark tragedy that lay so heavily inside me almost cracked under a sudden impulse to laugh. Without a word the children ran away; the news made it impossible for them to stand still.

'He was high up when I saw the mist coming over the hill. I was watching its advance so closely that I never noticed that the air was filling with it over my head. When I looked up to call Genghis down its whiteness had covered the sun—and the falcon too. Very soon I was completely enveloped in it. So was the whole moor.'

In her wish to offer consolation she reminded me that I had lost hawks before, but that I had nearly always got them back. But on this occasion, as I pointed out to her, Genghis was still fairly new to the moor and its surroundings. The mist would force him off the high ground and in the lowlands he was a complete stranger. It was useless to look for him down below because the mist had arrived there before I left. He would fly away from it all and I shall never see him again.

Little else was said between us and then she went in and closed the door. That simple act filled me with dull depression where previously there had been active despair. To go in and close the door. It has a clean finality about it that cuts through muddled thinking. The subject enters another dimension and communication is cut off. The full force of its significance reached me once when a woman spoke of the manner in which she had seen her son, shortly after his death. She saw him cross the landing of their home, looking happy, and then he walked into his room and closed the door. The act is so impersonal, it shows no sign of recognition of one's feelings, clearly defining the one side where there may be song and laughter and on the other mourning and tears, health and sickness, peace and war, time and eternity.

I went along on heavy feet to tell Robert about it all. He looked so sad that I could hardly restrain a slow smile of gratitude for his understanding. Beyond saying that we must be out at dawn what little else he added concerned only the means to be employed for Genghis's recovery. I said yes, yes, to his suggestions but felt no hope at all although I did not tell him so. Nevertheless apart from any scheming to get a lost hawk back, Robert is the best person to go to at such a time because you feel that there is something solid about him to hang on to. Where another person might empty the shallows of his mind in a lot of useless talk Robert just goes immensely thoughtful, and when the initial shock is over he lightens the situation with gems of sly humour. And of course being both of us falconers we speak the same language.

The hawks' weathering enclosure looked depressingly empty. The peregrines were there all right, but good as they are, for me they have faded into the background since all my enthusiasm had centred on Genghis. So the crown had been transferred to him, to Robert's secret disgust, for he is ever loyal to his peregrines, being sceptical of the gyr's vaunted fame. He considers me unfeeling and ungrateful, and wonders that I can apparently overlook the wonderful flights that have so often thrilled us when *Falco peregrinus* has taken the air. No, I have not forgotten, Robert. I can never forget the hundreds—no, thousands of miles we have walked and run through the heather in following her bells. Nor the mountains we have climbed nor the cliffs we have descended in search of the eyasses in the eyrie.

We have trained and flown eyasses, passagers and haggards, and in hunting with them have sweated in the heat and shivered in the cold when the gales of winter have sent even the wild hawks off the moor. And the dawns that we have seen in the search for lost hawks! The waiting in the darkness for sufficient light to put us on our way. Waiting to go out to be greeted later by a rising sun or driven on into misery by squalls. The straining of the ears to catch the distant tinkle of a bell. The despair when the wind's roaring shuts out all chance of hearing its melodious sound. The miles of moor to be searched. The hope of being back for breakfast, the growing fear as day wears on that the hawk is too far away. But, above all, the sudden thrill when the clean-cut form of a falcon stars the sky. The agonizing moment that decides whether she fly away as a wild hawk, or fly to us as a tame. And then the falconer's triumphant return with his falcon, that was lost, found at last! Failure or success, the whole allurement of falconry is in its never being wholly under the falconer's control. It does not surrender all its mysteries to him. He must lead his falcon to the outer edge of training, after that she largely leads him, and if she become impatient with his earthly limitations, if she fly higher than he can see or farther than he can go, he can hardly blame her even if he would.

To train and fly a hawk is just as much an adventure for a man of fifty as it is for a boy of fifteen. However old a falconer may become, in years, every time he takes a hawk on his fist the old excitement comes back again. The boy expects each hawk to be the best ever, of course, whereas experience has shown the man that the best performers are spread out rather thinly over the years, but whether hierofalco, the great gyrfalcon, open a new era for us or not, we shall never forget those living moments in pursuit of *Falco peregrinus*, how she has caused us to hunger and thirst on fears and disappointments as well as to feast on success.

Tomorrow we were to have hawked grouse. I had visualized my triumph with the gyrfalcon among my falconry friends upon the moor. They would stand round him, stowing away their awed admiration for his looks and making it appear by words that they expected little or nothing in the way of performance, and I would say nothing to lead them to suppose that I rated him any higher. He would be flown first and probably time would be lost in trying to recall a bird on erring wings. There would be general relief at his recovery so that, after his having 'let them down' they would cease wasting further time and thought on him, the discredited hierofalco, the broken myth, and turn again with thankfulness to the peregrine, the universal friend of falconers. After that there would be much high flying and hard stooping. The grouse would fly up in their coveys to speed over the purple heather, and the moor would ring with shouts of Hoo! Ha! Ha! the ancient hawking cry, and more than one grouse would be struck down dead to bounce off the heather. Then everything would stop for tea, and after tea I would prepare to fly the gyr again. With tongue in cheek I would strip him of his leash and swivel and in mock modesty and with mock diffidence crave my friends' indulgence, and they would patiently make ready for another gyr fiasco, politely remarking that at least there is interest in so rare a sight as a gyr on the wing, and even giving him credit for speed. Then the chatter would fade out with his taking the air. He would take their breath away with surprise at his steep ascent. He would go straight up on his tail where before the other falcons ascended in progressive spirals. Then would come his flowering in his greater command of the sky. Where the peregrines came down in measured stoop, falling, falling through the air to flatten out at the end of it as on the swing of a pendulum, the gyr on impetuous wings would drive the whole distance down and with far greater dash smack his grouse to the ground, and his towering throw-up taking him vertically on the rebound straight as an arrow high into the sky again would tell of the greater weight behind his stoop. Masterly would be his style and in the grand manner his whole performance. And in the days to come I would make a pretence of flying him only under the greatest reserve, keeping him in the background until all my friends' hawks had been flown. Only through pressure of my friends' entreaties would I finally yield and bring the master performer forward to take the air.

In moments of vision that is how I saw it all. I would bask in the praise of his superb flying as if I were the bird's own creator. Then after the day-dream came the shock, like a punch in the stomach, on the sudden reawakening to the fact that the gyr had been taken from me and my vanity punished. In times of crisis one instinctively seeks a way out through some sort of activity, if that be mental it does little or nothing for easement, but through physical exertion pain can be expelled from the mind. The gyr is lost, but there is nothing to suggest that he might be dead. He was cut off by mist, something had come in between him and me. If only I could get to him! I would walk scores of miles, endure fatigue and gladly undergo every lesson in humility if only the smallest chance still remains to find him. No amount of searching would ensure his recovery, it would not necessarily revive any hope, but at least it would prolong his last chapter. Theoretically it would indicate that the door is not quite closed.

The mist had not ended with the obscuring of the moor. I saw that its chill vengeance was bent on following me for it had reached the low-lying park. Soon it was advancing up the slopes towards us, and then the house, the cottage and finally the whole of our world was overtaken by it. When a hive of bees has been upset the intruder seeks escape by running away, but the bees follow and distance does not lessen the ferocity of their attack. Everywhere surrounded by mist; I suffered agony because all thought of going back to look for the gyr was abandoned. Nothing remained but torturing activity of mind that could do nothing to get him back. The early morning had been warm with sunshine but with the mist had come a fall in temperature and I could only wait in cold despair.

Perhaps the white enemy would resolve itself in the night. That is what Robert and I told each other when we planned to be out before dawn. When he went to bed it was as dense as ever outside. I promised to call him half an hour before the first light. Our both going to bed was out of the question because we might both over-sleep. Apart from that consideration I personally find it impossible to get a restful night in bed under such circumstances, for one lies half submerged but not properly in sleep. The alarm clock's bell cannot guarantee to wake one up, so, being afraid to yield to the seductive inner whispering of sleep that pulls one down completely, one drifts in semi-consciousness with one hand almost resting on the clock and the other on the switch for the light. On such occasions my only dream concerns the hands of the clock which seem disinclined to point to any time except that which startles the sleeper into wakefulness. The bed invites complete forgetfulness, so, being afraid to accept that invitation, I turn to the armchair that offers a dozey cosiness, and that rarely betrays by complete annihilation in sleep. There is less anxiety in resting with boots on in a subdued light with clock at elbow for company. In those circumstances it seems to blaze the time instead of making one play hide and seek with it on a bedside table in the dark. In any case it is hardly worth while going to bed because in three or four hours I must be up again.

For a night's sitting it is of course important that the armchair be a really comfortable one and such, in my experience, is hard to find. The seats of some are too high and so put a strain on one's back. Most of them have the arms too high so that either the sitter has to prop his elbows on the tops of them, in which enforced position he feels like a trussed chicken, or he has to squeeze them in between and so deprive himself of a supporting hand for the head. Another common fault is that the back of the chair is too straight, so that if the sitter fit his back into it he is not in a reclining position, and if in seeking this he plant his posterior forward the small of his back aches because it lacks support. Instead of correcting these defects most manufacturers attempt, with considerable success, to stifle objections with cloying upholstery and a magnificent display of generosity in regard to size. My own armchair is too modest to offer such an ostentatious invitation to repose, but when you sit in its lap there is genuine comfort in its dilapidated folds. In it one can float on the lightest and most pleasant of dreams or become a receiving station for those very special thoughts it attracts. It soothes and revives so that in peace one can come to terms with adversity. The gyrfalcon is lost, but now there is nothing to be done about it except to rest at one end of the night's quietness, while somewhere, on some far rock perhaps, he is at the other. During these hours that precede the dawn I cannot search for him and he can fly no farther, for the same dark hand holds us both down in inactivity.

The mist persisted and hid the breaking of the day. There was no need to awaken Robert, he could sleep on until breakfast time. With the return of day waiting became disturbingly active again whereas in the night it had been restfully passive. If only the mist would clear so that we could go out! There were moments when we began to see landmarks that had been previously hidden, but they became obscured again. Thus hope rose and fell. The white enemy mocked and left us in sullen misery.

In the afternoon a man arrived. He had come some twenty miles by road, but from his farm on one of the foothills at the far end of the moor it was no more than about twelve as the falcon flies. On the approach of his machine up the drive I had run out to meet him as, through restlessness, I had already done a dozen times when anybody arrived. In his case he did not reach the top of the hill because his machine broke down. He said it had done that at several stages on the journey, but he had pressed on and was glad that he had arrived because I might be interested to know that the previous evening a large falcon was on his farm. Had I lost a hawk? Well, yes, as a matter of fact I could not deny that I had, but what a pity he had not informed me yesterday evening, or last night, because I would have been at his farm this morning at dawn when it would have been easy to have collected it where it was roosting before it flew away again. Was the bird still at his place when he left? He could not rightly say but he had heard its bells before breakfast when he went to fetch the cows in. Well, it was exceedingly kind of him to take the trouble to come and report the incident. To cover his slight embarrassment at being thanked he began telling the story all over again, and Robert and I neither hurried him nor showed impatience because he was enjoying himself, and, after all he had left his work to travel forty miles to say what he was saying out of friendliness and because his desire to help was genuine.

Anyone hearing our conversation, the easy questioning

and the purring answers, might have thought that the subject under discussion was of no more than pleasant and passing interest. We might have been talking about some old gentleman who had been seen out strolling. But one thing stuck in my mind above all others, he said that he had heard the bells. From that moment they were ringing in my ears again. In imagination I was receiving their sound waves, myself at one end of them, the living falcon at the other. Had there been no fog, had the news been fresh, within the hour of his being seen, what a different state of affairs there would have been at home! It had happened before. A lost hawk had been seen, and everything that had been placed in readiness for any news coming in had been hastily grabbed and we had been away on the trail almost before the last word of the announcement had been spoken. But on this occasion the lapse of time had taken the edge off eagerness. The hawk's bells had been heard at 7 a.m. and it was now five o'clock in the afternoon. One could say with certainty that he had pushed on through the fog, the same fog that was drugging our minds and hindering our movement.

All the same our friend had gone to a lot of trouble. Clearly he expected some sort of action on our part and we were not going to disappoint him. Apart from that it really was rather a relief to be able to do something even though there was no hope attached to it. I was telling our visitor that he had better leave his machine behind for repairs, and come with Robert and me, when someone else was heard coming up the hill. He was our first arrival's close neighbour. I know him well, he is Mr. Evan Jones. A great, tall man he is, so tall that all his neighbours call him Evan Drip. He told us that he had had some doubt about Leonard's reaching us so he thought he had better come along himself.

'Well now,' I said, 'let's go, or shall we wait in case someone else turns up?' and to my surprise they laughed a sudden, uproarious laugh as if I had said something funny. Robert and I looked at each other in mutual declaration that from then on fun was to be the mood. At such a time when other people are ready to laugh at the least provocation one wants to laugh at their laughter, perhaps because one is stimulated by the change in mental outlook. By the time the car was brought round to the front anyone hearing us might have thought there was a hurrah party on by the noise we were making. They all got in while I got a rag out and wiped the windscreen clear. Then I took the driver's seat, and, looking over my shoulder at the passengers behind asked them questions about the route and the condition of the narrow road near their farms. Was the fog any worse for driving in their locality than what it was here? I pondered their answers and then, with a decisive movement, asked them if they were ready to go and they said they were, looking a little surprised at the question. Then I opened the door and got out, saying that if they were ready who was going to drive? They looked at each other and then asked me whether I was not going to drive. I said 'I can't'. They asked me what I meant.

'I just don't know how to,' I replied.

More roars of laughter.

'No, really I can't. I hate the vulgar, noisy, smelly things.'

'All the same you've got a very nice one,' one of them said, to which I replied that you've got to have one in self defence, and they shouted with laughter again.

When, after slow travelling, we finally arrived at the farm I jumped out, and, having put sufficient distance between myself and the house so as not to disturb the people unduly by violent whistling, I whistled on my referee's whistle, sending it shrilling far out into the mist until my head began to ache, but there was no answering tinkle of bells. Robert and I were not disappointed because we had not expected anything different. So we returned to the farm house and had a welcome cup of tea with the family by the kitchen fire. Before leaving I suggested to the two men that if the mist had cleared by the morning they might like to meet us up on the moor by Frogs' Gutter at eleven o'clock. They could come hawking with us. With a peregrine in the air it would be just conceivably possible we may see something of the gyrfalcon because the peregrine would attract him if he were anywhere within ten miles. On the conclusion of the afternoon's hawking they could return with us to my home where they could collect their machines. So it was agreed.

The friendliness of those people had so cheered us that Robert and I were feeling considerably better on our return. But better than anything else was the lifting of the mist that happened soon after nightfall. Now we really could plan to be out at dawn, refusing to contemplate that the enemy might return. Much later, by the time I had settled in the armchair for another upsitting, the night was calm and sparklingly clear. I felt relieved and content in the thought that the way was now open for us to go out in the morning on our search. That would be doing something, and after it would be over we could fly the peregrines with an easier mind in the knowledge that nothing further could be done on the gyrfalcon's account. By now I was gradually beginning to reconcile myself to the thought that he was something that had happened in the past. His training and subsequent flying had never been anything more than an experiment, an experiment that at one time had seemed so promising, yet, in the end, had failed, and I had been properly punished for my over-confidence. But, thank goodness, there were the faithful peregrines to turn to again. Robert had been right all along in not being led astray from them. It would be futile to continue to lament the gyr's loss and there is no cause to regret having had him because, however small the contribution, the experience with him has added a little to the store of knowledge on modern falconry. Probably he had no more wish to lose me than I him, but however that may be I will refuse to believe anything else than that he has returned to the wild and that the closing weeks of winter will find him on his way up to the Arctic again.

It must have been about a couple of hours after midnight as I sat, thinking thus, in the depths of the armchair. It was the very heart of the night when time seems to have run out, when even those unfortunates who hardly sleep at all pass through a brief unconsciousness. A silence of great intensity had enveloped everything. It so affected me that it became an effort to determine whether I was breathing or not. Then I heard something. It did not happen suddenly and I hardly know whether the disturbance, if such it was, came from within or without. Someone was approaching and the footfalls were so indeterminate that I did not even open my eyes to them. He was coming along the corridor and I knew, during his approach, that he would stop outside my door, and he did. Then I opened my eyes and watched the door-handle, expecting to see it turn. Whoever it was on the other side, could he have seen me, would have seen only the vacuous stare in my face, the expressionless gaze that watching and waiting leave behind. It was utterly impossible for me to move yet I felt no restriction of paralysis. Far from being afraid I wished intensely that he would enter. I was here, he was there, and only the thickness of the door divided us, a division so slight that we were as good as together, yet so definite that neither of us could have any claim on the other. Nevertheless he paused outside the doorway, through which, had it been willed, he would have entered to join me, but he did not, he passed on instead. At the sound of his retreating footsteps I longed to call him back again but was incapacitated to do so. When he had gone I knew for a certainty that he would never return.

If you say that the experience was nothing more than a dream I will not bother to deny it. Whether it was or not is relatively unimportant, but something did happen; that I do not doubt; and I remembered my dream about pierrots. Its recollection, up on the moor, only brought a vague uneasiness that lovely morning when Genghis first flew free. Now I perceived its full import, for the long white line of them was of course the advancing mist that bore down on me and robbed me of my hawk.

Not only dreams influence daily life for it seems that the upper strata of consciousness is penetrated by signs and portents that can disturb mental associations with things we cherish. So did uneasiness flare up in me after I awoke on the morning of the day I lost Genghis.

I had turned away from the early morning tea-tray that lay on my bedside table and was lying against the pillows, going through a mental list of the day's intentions warmed outwardly by the sun, that streamed through the open window, and inwardly by the tea, when the door opened and, to my surprise, the housemaid entered carrying a breakfast tray. I did not know where she had got her information that I wanted breakfast in bed because I had not ordered it, and my bedroom is easily identifiable, but there she was. On raising her eyes to my recumbent form she hesitated. Suddenly the possibilities inside the gleaming silver dish-cover she carried became immense.

A woman walking about in an irresponsible manner with a breakfast tray is a wasted potentiality for good, a dissipation of beneficial power that ought to be harnessed.

'Yes, thank you, I'll take it!' I called to her as she was about to turn away, but she only bared her teeth by way of a smile.

'Now that you've brought it in don't take it away again!' Surely the justification for that order was overwhelming.

'Don't go away! Come back!' and I stretched out my arms in a detaining gesture, for she had already reached the door.

'I am ill! I need sustenance!'

She turned in the doorway, still smiling, the white on her exposed strip of teeth matching the impeccable whiteness of her starched head-dress.

'Look here,' I said. 'If you are going probing all round the rooms with that tray you may as well leave it here because this is where it is really needed.'

But I never got so much as a *tra-la-la* from her, for, still smiling, she backed out and closed the door.

She closed the door. If she had only left it ajar I would have seen there an invitation, or maybe a provocation, to have leapt out of bed and in a mad rush overhaul and foul-hook the tray, and that would have been better sport than casting for it by word of mouth from the bed. In righteous anger I would have demanded whether she abandoned me as an act of cold denial, or indeed did open defiance take the place of charity? Had she, in her duplicity, exhibited a pretended misdirection, an error of judgment, on my side of the door, and did her face unmask to reveal mischievous design on the other? Did her feet, wandering apparently where they listed, take a frivolous hop, skip and a jump after she had wantonly made me a victim of her flibberty-gibberty caprice?

But she closed the door and, in a daze, I accepted defeat, seeing only that gleaming dish-cover that had been waved so tantalizingly before me.

I feel a terrible sick certainty that I will never see Genghis again.

An hour before daybreak I made tea. While the kettle was boiling I went outside and saw that the night was beautifully clear. Oddly enough, after drinking the tea I felt in splendid form and very much alive, conscious of an inner, inexplicable excitement. A cup of tea in such unusual circumstances, on the brink of the first day of the hawking season, might have had some connection with my elation, but there was more in it than that. I put another cup and the teapot on a tray and took it up to Robert. Within half an hour we were up on the moor.

On our arrival the stars had hardly begun to pale so we set our backs against the cottage wall and waited, but the silence was soon broken by the guttural talking of an old cock grouse and then they all began to call 'Go back!' all over the moor, just as they had done before the rising of the sun for thousands of years. For a time we listened to them, and then we ourselves began to talk about inconsequential things until real conversation took shape around the day's hawking ahead. We reviewed the respective merits of the two falcons, Donna and Infanta, whom Robert had been exercising daily for the past three weeks in preparation for the opening of the season. They were good hawks, as good perhaps as any that had been flown over these ancient lands during the centuries when Welsh chieftains hawked here, as later did kings of England after the moor became a royal forest. As we talked the wind blew freshly in our faces. It was bringing up the dawn and we were getting restless. When we could see individual cock grouse springing up out of the heather, on their short display flights, we had received our signal. We knew then that it was time to go. He went one way and I went another. We had arranged to meet again at Frogs' Gutter at nine o'clock when we would return for breakfast and afterwards bring up the hawks.

I heard Robert's whistling but I held my own until the increasing distance between us made his nearly inaudible and then I began to blow mine, and as I walked I swung the lure. I walked to the summit of every hill on each of which I stayed for five minutes whistling and luring. From these points of vantage a lost hawk, many miles away, could have seen me. Had it been attracted to Robert's lure, instead, the arrangement was that he would keep it on the wing as near him as possible by means of much luring while running hard in my direction until the hawk catch sight of me when it would be my responsibility to call it down.

On these occasions one frequently imagines one hears the distant tinkling of bells. They draw one on and they multiply until the silence is filled with their pretty deception. A mirage of the mind perhaps or are they the shadowy language of unearthly things? Falconers all seem to have this experience when out searching for a hawk in lonely places and it is understandable that, for them, 'hearing things' should take that form. And then the senses are so sharpened that every wild hawk that shows itself against the sky for one exciting moment appears as the one that is lost. Expectancy leads the falconer on and makes him tireless and forgetful of time, nothing escapes his attention. Any unusual behaviour on the part of bird or beast is noted. A crow cawing protestingly in the branches of a distant mountain ash may indicate that a hawk is feeding on its kill somewhere near. A flock of sheep or herd of wild ponies, that are seen suddenly to lift their heads, may have been startled by a large bird with bells attached flying over them. Every such happening must be investigated. A walk of this kind is never dull, for, above all things, it has purpose. It keeps one continually on the alert and sharpens observation. Pity the poor town dweller who walks in suburban surroundings on hard pavement simply for the sake of exercise, rarely able to rid himself of the sight of bricks and mortar! On this morning I wandered over a moor that had no disfigurement of house or building anywhere on its miles and miles of rolling uplands, except the funny little cottage known as Frogs' Gutter, and that seems anxious to hide itself in its screen of stunted, wind-twisted trees. In all the considerable distance I walked I saw no human being, wishing for no better company than those denizens of the heather, the wild red grouse, and the curlews, snipe, skylarks, wheatears, ring ouzels, kestrels, merlins, plover and the little meadow-pipits whose distant tinkling notes are so suggestive of hawk bells. Up here one is conscious of freedom that gives lightness to the feet as they go over the springy heather so that walking is no effort. Sometimes I surprised a sheep in a hollow in the heather and it would run off a little distance to turn and face its intruder and stamp its foot and whistle down its nose. I wondered how long they would be allowed to roam in peace up here. One day would see them in some noisy, crowded market place. How many of the buyers would pause in front of the pens, in contemplation, to contrast such close confinement within iron railings with their former freedom? How many would try to picture the fairyland of sheltered glens, of lively, hurrying mountain streams, pebbly beaches and surprising waterfalls, of crystal-clear pools half hidden in the bends and the fingerling trout that dart within them? What scenes of exquisite beauty those mountain sheep, penned in markets, must have known! 'Straight off the hills!' is the oft repeated cry of recommendation that is calculated to rouse the buyers' interest, but it is a declaration of the animals' fitness to fatten and not the romance of their recent wandering that the salesman would invoke.

There are half-forgotten valleys in this moor. One has to go out of the way to find them and when you enter one it is a discovery that makes one feel an intruder. In spring-time especially they guard such loveliness that they would appear to deny the right to be there except one enter in reverent mood, and then there is a welcome in them for erring, twentieth-century man. He is greeted by the singing of ring-ouzels, a rare bird in ordinary places, but here they are everywhere among the lichen-painted rocks and the delicate unfolding green of birch and rowan. When the sun shines in these trees and the breeze stirs the glitter in their leaves the whole place sparkles with light. Through it all the ring-ouzels sing and when you have descended to the basin of the valley you find water-ouzels harmonizing their water-music with the burbling of the brook. Many a time I have sat there inhaling the hot-sweet smell of flowering gorse, for a smell it is and not a perfume, being too robust for that, matching in strength the pleasant pungency of sheep. In its furzy fastness linnets sing, but not a song that competes with the ouzels'. There are usually scores of them singing but the ears are not assailed by it. So much does it lull the mind in drowsed contentment that a stranger to the country probably would not notice it. Only an ear trained in country sounds can fully appreciate the harmony of that sweet whispering that is so peculiarly their own.

These sheltered valleys are often favoured by a lost hawk. By taking note of the wind's direction it is sometimes possible to anticipate in which one she will pass the night, that is to say of course if the falconer have reason to suppose she has not left the moor, and that is unlikely if she be old in training. Many times, after a hawk has killed a grouse and we have been unable to find her on it, I have arrived at the chosen valley first, to see her come flying in with the last of the daylight. With a full crop on her she has yet sometimes allowed me to take her up, other times she prefers to pass the night amid the shelter of the rocks like a wild hawk. Hawkham Hollow—Hawks' Home—is the name of one of these little-known valleys. Falconers of bygone centuries found it to be a favourite retreat for the hawks that they had left out, as it is especially sheltered from the wind, and they named it accordingly. We their descendants find that in this respect, as in all others, hawks have not changed their habits. Many times I have noted a hawk's arrival there and have returned before dawn to see her come flying to meet me before the morning stars had gone. In recent years however I have trained my hawks to return to Frogs' Gutter which they have been very willing to do.

To search for a lost hawk at break of day may appear a depressing business. It is not an occasion one would choose on which to ask a non-falconer to accompany one to see this aspect of falconry, particularly if the weather be wild and stormy. The thought of rousing a visitor in his bed, with nothing more than a lighted candle to lend reality to the invitation, does indeed open up possibilities. If he protest at the intrusion one could take refuge in the plea of anxiety to entertain and he could not deny its novelty. It would be fun to see him roll his eyeballs in horror towards the night's blackness on the windowpane and uncover an ear to the howling of the wind outside. Before he could regain any sort of composure in the shadow of his night's disturber I would gravely shake my head in announcing extreme doubt over the chance of returning in time for breakfast. Perhaps such a scene was commonly enacted when falconry ruled the world of sport, it might even have inspired the famous lines:

T'was the voice of the sluggard,
I heard him complain
'You have woke me too soon,
I must slumber again'.

but I think it is somewhat doubtful whether a genuine falconer would issue such an invitation, because when there is a lost hawk to be recovered he is then least disposed to turn aside to make the event an occasion for popular pleasantries.

I once had a falcon which I named Aurora, Goddess of the Dawn, because she and I so frequently held rendezvous in the early hours. She enjoyed so much liberty, of her own taking, that she followed closely the wild hawk's daily habits, being well aware of the ease with which she could obtain her own living. Nevertheless although she loved her freedom she showed no inclination to break off her friendship with man. It was a delightful partnership and I forgave her all the anxiety I endured on her behalf. I forgave her too for so frequently cutting so short my nights of sleep. Dawn after dawn would see me out on the moor looking for her. Sometimes the weather was fine and I would step out with a mixed feeling of exhilaration and hope. Sometimes there were gales, sometimes it rained and, because she did not like me in a raincoat, I got soaked to the skin. There were even times when I sought her in a snowstorm. Conditions were sometimes so bad when the weather put up every possible barrier between her and me that I was constrained to exclaim 'This is the end of Aurora!' In despair I would push on with lowered head against the storm, guided by nothing in particular, and then suddenly depression would be dashed out of my mind by the sound of her bells, and before I could give thanks she would be at my feet, looking fearlessly into my face with her splendid, shining eyes. There were occasions when thick mist blanketed everything, when I could not walk but only stand and blow the whistle, and yet she has followed up the course of its sound until she found me. At all times on arrival she voiced a cry of joy. Aurora! what ample cause she gave me to associate her with the dawn! Almost always I was able to carry her back in good time for breakfast, but afterwards there followed all too frequently the same train of events. I would go out hawking with her in the afternoon when, glorying in flight, she would ascend into the sky and remain up there sometimes out of sight, so that it was visually impossible to tell whether she was following the hawking party and the dogs which ranged over the heather. But I knew that she was there all right. It only needed a covey of grouse to rise and fly away to prove that she had had her keen eyes on the proceedings all the time. To shouts of 'Where's the hawk?' for answer there always came a disturbance in the air above. It first came to the ear like a far-away sigh that quickly resolved itself into a great rushing sound as she annihilated the distance between sky and earth. Hardly were the flying grouse warned of their terrible danger before she cut right through the whole pack of them, leaving one behind, dead, on the ground, slain to all appearances by nothing more than the passing touch of her foot. It was one of the most superbly dramatic performances in nature that, ordinarily, man is so seldom privileged to see. The trouble was that we did not see its consummation often enough for, as likely as not, some grouse would get up beyond our horizon, disturbed by a passing shepherd perhaps, and the hawk, having command of the whole moor by reason of the great height at which she waited-on over our heads, would stoop and kill her bird out of sight. Sometimes after a search lasting up to an hour we found her on the remains of the grouse, but often we did not, and when we were unlucky she was left out for another night, which meant yet another dawn rendezvous with her.

When war came and I had to go away I left Aurora in the charge of Robert who, at that time, was still too young to join up. She knew him well but there was something about him that she did not trust. As a falconer he understands and handles his hawks better than I ever could, yet she never gave him her confidence; whether it was because she disliked his blond hair I do not know. However that may be she always flew off with her prey on his approach, whereas she was always pleased to see me, being very ready to leave the dead grouse to jump to my fist. The first time he flew her after my departure she went her own way, and though she remained on the moor for many weeks afterwards she never allowed him to take her up. She flew only for me, so because I was not there she ceased to act as a trained hawk and became a wild one.

In those days grouse were plentiful on the moor but the same cannot be said now. Three bad seasons have prevented any increase. Plenty of young birds were hatched last spring, but cold winds and successive days of rain killed them. They were all old birds that I saw during my dawn wandering and they were wild for the time of year. When I met Robert again at the end of our search the first words I spoke were to ask him if he had seen any young birds and he said no. It was plain that the question struck him as oddly out of order for scarcely was it out of my mouth when, all eagerness, he shot one at me. 'Had I seen any sign of him?' he asked, the stress in his face reproving me for my apparent indifference to the purpose of our visit.

'No, Robert,' I replied. 'I have not, neither have you. Neither of us will ever see him again. Our coming out this morning has been nothing more than a farewell gesture to him. From now on we forget him and think only of Donna and Infanta. You were right all the time, it's better to stick to peregrines.'

Genghis had made his entry through the mists of the land of trolls, and he had departed in mist which was a fitting medium for his conveyance since he was enshrouded in the mystery that tradition has created, and which the light of modern knowledge has done little to dispel in its application to the genus hierofalco.

CHAPTER VII

We returned to breakfast with glowing cheeks for the cold dawn wind had been spirited. Very high up crowds of little white clouds were sailing the sky in regatta. The atmosphere was conducive to gaiety, having a briskness in it that smacked of autumn. For that we were thankful because languor and heat do not go well with a day's hawking. When it is hot grouse seek shade in the areas of deep bracken where they are hard to find, the dogs become listless and the hawks get their mouths open, showing that they are in no condition for flying.

On the opening day of the hawking season Robert and I feel that it is unlucky to have a crowd of followers. One or two friends at the most are allowed, even encouraged, but when a lot of people swarm over the moor proceedings are apt to get noisy and out of control. Grouse get up at the wrong time and in the wrong places and consequently hawks fly badly.

To seek the quiet we need we usually leave home and go to live for a time at Frogs' Gutter, arriving there one or two days before the season opens. However, this year, unfortunately, we were prevented from doing so. The move up there has been delayed, but as soon as circumstances permit we shall be up there with one or two friends, happily isolated in a small cottage, right in the middle of the moor and miles from anywhere. There we live the simple life, it is rather like camping out with a roof over our heads.

After a late breakfast I did not find it so easy to get away. First one thing and then another contrived to delay me and I kept nervously looking at my watch, mindful of the meeting that had been arranged on the moor with our friends the two farmers. It did not help matters when people began to turn up, local friends and acquaintances. They appeared to have all the time in the world and failed to appreciate that I was too occupied to want to stop and talk with them. 'Are you going hawking today? Do you mind if we come with you?' I seemed to be hearing those questions every ten minutes and could only reply that it all depended on whether I could get away. So they hung around in front of the house and I saw with alarm that their numbers grew. Robert kept putting his head round the door to ask if I was ready. It was not really a question but a reminder to me to hurry, and as I was already doing that to the point where patience was beginning to wear a bit thin I disliked the look of his face the more I saw of it. When it appeared about the fifth time I verbally swiped it by telling him that we should have to call the whole thing off.

'Take the hawks back to the weathering ground,' I ordered. 'Convey my apologies to the ladies and gentlemen outside and say that Mr. Stevens regrets he's unable to hawk today.'

He knew of course that I longed to go as much as he did and that my outburst was only the measure of my exasperation at being held back, and he knew one other thing and that was that he had better keep out of my way.

But of course he was not in the least put out and very soon I saw him, through the window, in the centre of the crowd of people, and I smiled to myself to see how he was holding all their attention, and how good-humoured and pleased they were to have him among them. There is neither man, woman, nor child round here who has not got the greatest liking for Robert. He would do nothing to encourage them up here, but as they had arrived he was very ready to make the best of a situation that neither of us wanted, while I, in no good mood, was trying to straighten out the sag in my face, in the background, preparatory to advancing on them and apologizing for the delay.

Then I stood on the portico steps facing my visitors, undecided whether to assume an appearance of simple gaiety or try something more advanced like laughing with tears in my eyes. However, if they were waiting for me to say something Robert was not, for suddenly he appeared under me and automatically I drew the gauntlet on to my left hand and then received from him the hooded falcon Infanta. Then he and I led the way. As we passed through the village people waved to us from their gardens and I could not help regretting that we were not mounted on horseback as were bygone hawking parties whose trail we followed.

When we arrived on the moor our friends the two farmers were there waiting for us, so too, alas! were friends of theirs! It would have been troublesome to count how many there were of us altogether, but certainly we were the greater part of a large number. We started off from Quarry Hill which is a mile beyond Frogs' Gutter. Robert slipped the setter and before we had gone very far the dog pointed.

In case my reader is unfamiliar with the sport of hawking I had better explain, at this point, that early in the season grouse can be expected to lie, crouched in the heather, to the point of a dog. (A dog is said to point when he freezes into a statuesque attitude on scenting game.) When the dog thus indicates the presence of grouse, which of course are hidden from sight, it is the signal for the falconer to unhood his hawk and cast her off his fist. She then flies round in wide circles, ascending all the time, until she has gained a good height over the watching people below. When, by a few short turns and the suspended beating of her wings, she shows that she is ready for the field below to play their part, a spaniel is sent in to flush the grouse. These birds then spring into flight and in a matter of seconds are disappearing into the distance at a speed of sixty miles an hour, considerably faster when they have a stiff wind behind them. On sighting them the hawk appears to shoot forward, she then turns over and launches herself into an earthward dive that enables her to overtake them with ease so that in no time she is down on a level with them and passing through the covey at such speed that the birds appear to be flying slowly by comparison. No sooner has she passed through them than she is shooting up skywards again on the rebound from her lightning descent, but not without leaving a dead grouse below her in the heather, struck down by a passing, slashing blow from her hind talons that is delivered all too quickly for the human eye to see in detail. That is how the falcon kills, and in her creation everything about her has been shaped for that end. She is built for speed. Every line, every curve of her body tells of that.

Robert had unleashed the falcon Donna, but before he had time to unhood her some of the spectators, in their eagerness, had edged forward too close on the pointing dog. As a result of their untimely approach, and of my warning shout to keep them back, the grouse, a barren pair, jumped into flight prematurely and away they went, while those people in the field who understood something of the procedure of hawking groaned audibly. In a few seconds the birds had disappeared out of sight.

With careless despair at so miserable a beginning I told Robert to unhood his hawk and let her go, so at the least she would be in the air on the next occasion when grouse would fly, whether by accident or design.

Some hawks ascend in fairly close circles, others like to take quarter- or half-mile sweeps over the moor while gaining the upper air. Generally speaking the better and more dashing a flier a hawk is the wider she flies. But Donna has developed her own way of mounting and this she now demonstrated by turning her tail towards us and flying clean away straight off downwind out of sight. I knew that we should have to allow her a few minutes before she would return in a straight line, climbing into the wind towards us, and one or two of our friends knew of this trick of hers, but it was amusing to see the majority of the field watching with open-mouthed disappointment as she flew away. It looked so absolutely final.

'She's gone! She's lost!' they cried.

Since they had scared away the grouse at which she should have flown I did not feel inclined to contradict them, so that when they looked to me to confirm their fears I only slowly shook my head in extreme seriousness and said that I did not suppose we should see her again for months and months and months. I passed my cigarette case round and exasperated them by banal remarks about the weather, leaving them in mute astonishment to wonder why I was not cross with such terrible loss. The funny part about it was that I really did begin to get a bit anxious when, after five minutes, she still had not returned. I had noted with uneasiness that the wind had been freshening, and this, after all, was her first real flight of the season. It was just conceivably possible that she really had wandered off. Then came Robert's voice calmly announcing that she was on her way back again. His eyesight is uncommonly good and always he spots a distant hawk before anyone else. An audible sigh of relief passed over the crowd as the distant speck against the sky gradually resolved itself into the returning falcon. She was flying high but not high enough. The wind must be blamed for that, though after a week's hawking her condition will be so improved that a wind such as blew this day would only exhilarate her into flying higher than usual.

We continued on our way with the hawk in the air above us, but as the minutes went by she began to show signs of fatigue, allowing herself to drift a hundred yards and more behind the advancing field, and, what is worse, losing height. The same wind that made her deviate from her correct position also made the grouse wild, though doubtless the ceaseless chatter of the field further frightened them. When the setter pointed, a hundred yards ahead, a score or more of arms were raised in his direction and this sudden movement put to flight another brace of grouse before we were ready for them. Had our friends kept their zeal under control we might have got round the crouching grouse and flushed them downwind. Now, of course, they flew hard in the wrong direction, and the hawk, at no great height and being unable to stoop against the wind, simply gave chase and hopeless chase it was. Grouse can outfly a peregrine against a stiff wind, and this pair, with the great start they had, easily made their get-away. Two or three seconds before Donna reappeared after her abortive chase yet another barren pair got up wild, and the falcon, catching sight of them, quickly disappeared again after them over the brow of the hill.

'Well, Robert,' I said. 'Not a very brilliant start to the hawking season!'

How bored he looked, and how I shared his feelings! To the crowd of onlookers who pressed round us with a 'What next?' look in their faces I said:

'Very, very tiresome, indeed!'

'Is she lost? Will she come back?' they asked; to which I replied:

'One thing is certain, she'll never catch that grouse because she is not yet in condition. Another week of flying would have made all the difference. But now she's gone.' And once again I produced a cigarette case and they all went very quiet.

We sat around in the heather for a quarter of an hour, and then I told Robert to return to Frogs' Gutter and take her down to the lure. It was his suggestion, for we both agreed that it was far more likely than not that she had got disgusted with the whole proceeding so had returned to the cottage to rendezvous with him there.

When he had gone I told the others that he had started off on a pretty hopeless quest for his lost hawk. I said this with the secret intention that the ennui of the afternoon should be relieved by his early dramatic return with her on his fist. After all, they had to be provided with entertainment of some sort, and to keep up their spirits I told them that I had been holding back the really good hawk, the star performer, until the end, and after we had rested for a little longer we would fly her on the other side of the moor. Some of them considerately begged me not to fly her just for them, against my better judgment. It appeared that they were fast becoming convinced that a hawk had but to leave the fist for it to fly away. I told them that, even though it may mean the loss of both, still I would fly Infanta. The show must go on.

So when Robert reappeared over the skyline without Donna I felt properly paid back for my foolish confidence. True, he had seen her, but up at a vast height and beyond recall because she was in combat with a wild falcon! The last he saw of her, he said, she was frantically trying to shift from the stoops of her attacker. The two birds were drifting downwind and were well off the moor and that was the last he saw of them.

It seemed so entirely profitless standing there talking of disaster, so I urged everybody to march since diversion was badly needed. We changed direction and had gone about a quarter of a mile when I chanced to see the head of an old cock grouse sticking up out of the heather, for a second, and then the bird crouched. We were far too close on it and the wonder was that it did not fly away, but by making signs of extreme supplication I persuaded the crowd not only to halt but to retreat from the vital spot. We retired in such good order that a rise in the ground soon hid us from the grouse. Then we began to talk again, to plan a new approach. We must make a detour so that we could advance on the grouse with the wind against our backs. This time the quarry *must* fly downwind. The people must be shown that a trained hawk can kill game, otherwise they would wonder what we are playing at.

And so we got ready. I drew the leash out of Infanta's swivel, and the swivel out of her jesses, then unhooded her. She was free to fly but they never do fly immediately, preferring to sit on the glove and leisurely take in the scene. When trained hawks have flown for several seasons, as Infanta and Donna have done, they understand and anticipate the falconer's every move, and not only his but the dogs' also. It is amusing to see how good-humouredly they regard the dogs and how, at times, they love to tease them by flying over their backs and flipping their ears in passing. Apart from the sport they give, and the wonderful power of flight they demonstrate, falcons make delightful pets, although that is a horrid word to use on a creature for whom one has immense respect.

It is curious how certain townsfolk who know only little about hawks presuppose that a falcon looks fierce, whereas in reality the opposite is the case. The bird's eyes, for its size, are large, dark and serious. They have an engaging honesty, but of ferocity there is none. They are as noble and as gentle as those of the rabbit-hunting spaniel. Just because a falcon preys on other birds to get her daily living some ignorant people imagine that she is savage in all her ways. 'Don't they ever go for you?' is a question that only reveals how entirely out of touch a person can be with the world of nature. Parrots and gaudy macaws bite the fingers in treachery, but nothing less than self-defence would make a peregrine behave similarly, she would have to be driven to it.

Infanta shook all her feathers and opened her wings to their full extent. She leant her body forward horizontally and the wind caught the undersides of her wings and relieved my fist of her two and a half pounds' weight. For a moment she poised herself thus and then by the lightest of pressures of her feet on the glove she was airborne and away, speeding over the heather. We watched her go, saw her mounting against the wind and flying in half-mile circles round us. To the spectators it might have been a matter for wonder that a falcon, ordinarily one of the wildest of creatures, should fly in any direction except away from man. Yet there she was, all the time measuring the distance from us as if no other thought could enter her head than to play her part rightly by us. She could fly clean away and get her own living if she chose, and well she knows it, yet her conduct proves that she asks for nothing better than to live with man and his dogs and to hunt in co-operation with him. Beyond doubt she appreciates the cheers of encouragement that come up to her from the falconer every time that game is sprung, and when she has killed a grouse or woodcock, partridge, duck or teal, is she pleased when her human partner approaches her, praises her and takes her on his fist? I am sure she is for she evinces every sign of satisfaction.

Voices were beginning to be raised impatiently among the watching people. 'Come on!' they shouted, 'she's high enough now. Let's run in and put the grouse up!'

'No, no! Not yet!' whispered Robert at my elbow. 'She hasn't finished mounting yet!' and of course he was right, for Infanta had not yet reduced the radius of her circling. He was waiting, as was I, for that certain short turn, that momentary resting on her wings that was her way of communicating to her friends below that she was ready for men and dogs to do their duty.

Still she climbed, up and up she went. She was little more than a speck in the heavens now, and at times that speck became obscured as it passed through little puffs of cloud. I remarked to Robert how the old girl was evidently enjoying herself and he replied out of the side of his mouth that she probably wanted to lose sight of some of the faces in the crowd.

As she had reached a height that was more than high enough for a killing stoop I waved the field on, anticipating that on her seeing the movement below she would break her circling and arrive over our heads and be in position for a stoop just at the moment when we should have reached the patch of heather that held the grouse. However, the manœuvre was not carried out, for suddenly we all halted again, having seen something that we did not like at all. Infanta had broken her circling, but not to come in to us, no, she went off in a straight line exactly in the opposite direction, flying away from us as hard as she could go.

There were groans from everyone. So this was the finish of a disastrous day's hawking! Voices rose loudly in complaint:

'We should have run in before! You left her up too long!' and guiltily I began to feel that they were right. Then the reason for her unexpected behaviour suddenly became clear.

'It's Donna!' shouted Robert, 'Donna that she's after!' and we could see now that there were two dots in the sky where previously there had been one.

Among the crowd several pairs of field-glasses were raised in the direction of the rapidly converging birds, who, on meeting, rose vertically and hung in the air crabbing at each other, and from very far away we could just hear the faint screams of combatant hawks.

Evidently, after her brush with the wild falcon beyond Frogs' Gutter, Donna had been on the way back, meaning to continue hunting with us, and now each hawk was angry on finding unexpectedly that she had a competitor in the air. There are instances where two falcons can be persuaded to fly together as a cast, but between these two there was bitter rivalry, so that we had long ago given up all hope of flying them together effectively.

The falcons drifted farther away, fighting as they went. Then again the unexpected happened, for instead of completely disappearing out of sight they all at once broke off combat, and one of them turned and began a return flight in our direction. This was a decided improvement in the situation. We could all begin to hope again. After all it now looked as if we should be able to show our friends a performance that they had come out to see, that is to say a flight at a grouse with a kill at the end of it, if indeed after all this excitement and delay the grouse was still there, for well might it have crept away to safety in the bracken that everywhere encroached upon the moor.

I saw Robert relieve a man of his field-glasses, saw him raise them to take a look at the second hawk who now, barely discernible in the distance, was moodily soaring at a tremendous height.

'Come on, Robert!' I called to him. 'What difference does it make? We've got one hawk over us. Let's go and put up that grouse before anything else happens!'

He came running up to me and I thought he looked a bit queer.

'Take a look!' he said.

I focused the glasses on the far-away hawk and when it came into view I felt a tingling sensation such as one feels when the thin, wavering, screaming whistle of a distant but onrushing train electrifies the senses. It is an eerie inkling that something stupendous is on its way, a dragon frighteningly at large speeding from the ends of earth, inexorably committed to single out its victim, to engulf one on that little plot of railway platform from which there is no escape in all the world's immensity. It has its counterpart in that state of mind wherein something hidden, some dark secret borne on tumultuous thinking rushes to its revelation, or where memory speeds along the track of years, where nostalgia's string of brilliantly lit but empty dreams flash by, a ghost train from the past.

We ran in excited disorder, a laughing and a noisy crowd transported by the magic that hawking releases so unexpectedly and that has the power to make men forget everything else. We raced each other round the rise in the ground and our good-humoured scrambling in the heather brought us to the place where the grouse should be. Not one but two got up and they startled us to a halt as they sped like twin bullets down the slope towards the valley. A hiss in the air above warned us of Infanta's stoop and we hardly had time to raise our eyes to it before she cut the hen grouse down in a cloud of feathers with a loud smacking blow. The hawk recovered herself from her throw-up and in less time than it takes to write this she was down in the heather on the dead bird. Then, to my horror, some of the people ran forward to the kill in their excitement and frightened the hawk away. In the confusion I heard another yell:

'Look!' they shouted.

It was not the cavalierly treated Infanta that they minded; she, poor bird, just ceased to exists for every man had riveted his attention on the sky across which the second hawk came slanting through sunlight in one tremendous stoop. She was miles away one moment and then was cutting through the next at a speed which put to naught the laws of space and time. And then again my mind was filled with the rushing of a speeding train, but this time one that had arrived. I stiffened and half-closed my eyes against the dazzling light through which she flashed. She tore over our heads in destructive splendour and caught up with the second grouse which then was far ahead. The lie of the land hid the end of the falcon's stoop but we saw her grand and stately throw-up that swung her vertically upwards, over the kill, far into the sky again.

I had seen enough and was off, running as hard as I could in the direction of the kill, and when I had outdistanced my pursuers I turned to face them and with spread arms implored them to stand fast. I felt that I was trying to hold back the twentieth century that in its mad rush would trample over falconry. Then I turned my back on them and dared to look at the shining form of Genghis who looked almost luminously pale against the heather.

There was uproar from the crowd and then Robert, whom I saw out of the corner of my eye despite my concentration, appealed for quiet and the noise died down to individual voices saying 'Genghis! It's Genghis!' It all takes on a different meaning as it comes back to me now, but clearest of all in that background is the memory of Robert, who, when he had finally succeeded in bringing about absolute silence and immobility among the people present, paced up and down, forming a barrier between them and me. He and I had but a single thought and that was that Genghis', temporary return to a feral existence might have infected him with wildness.

Whether the gyr had fed early in the day I cannot say, but he seemed in no hurry to deplume the dead grouse. For an awful moment I was tortured by the fear that he might fly away again and that his standing there by me was no more than a simple how-do-you-do. What was he waiting for? But there was no fear in his eye, only friendliness, and then he greeted me with the same throaty chuckle, his welcome that formerly I had become accustomed to, and courage came back to me. I touched his prey to attract his attention to it and he put his head down as if seeing it for the first time. Casually he began to deplume it. I searched my pocket for meat, put a piece into my gloved left hand, and without a moment's hesitation he stepped on to my fist. When he began to feed I put a swivel into his jesses and then pulled a leash through the swivel while the sweat ran down my face. He was safe.

I turned to my falconer in triumph. What unspeakable relief! And then Robert began to talk to the others in his quiet way while I stood aside feeding Genghis on my fist. The voice I heard was in a soft Scottish dialect. It was a recitation in monotone. He harked back to the fight between Donna and the wild peregrine above Frogs' Gutter, but what he then took to be a wild peregrine he was certain now was the lost gyrtiercel, the same that intruded in the last flight and that we mistakenly thought was the returning Donna. The hawking party continued to listen in silence while he recounted how he identified the gyr by his greater size after the two hawks had fought above us. What Robert saw with naked eye I beheld, scarcely believing, through field-glasses, but it was the gyr's pale underside that first excited my attention and even then I was not convinced that it was anything else than a trick of light aided by the great distance, and as for size there are some peregrines larger than others. Nevertheless there had been that queerness in my falconer's manner, that, and what I saw myself, had filled me with a premonitory thrill that was far short of straightforward recognition. If there had been any doubt about his identity, said Robert to his audience, the gyr's manner of intervention, his superior speed and style, were unmistakable when, immediately following on Infanta's kill, he had swept the sky and launched himself into that stoop that had so dramatically delivered him into our midst.

Robert never talks for the sake of talking and when he had finished all that he had to say other voices came in again. The saga of the gyrfalcon's return had been ably dealt with and it only remained now to return to the world of practical affairs. The pressing need of course was to recover the two peregrines that were still at large. One of them might have driven the other off the moor, or they both might have wandered away, and I think the latter was the general impression. However, Robert and

I knew that it was far more likely that they were both, at that moment, waiting for us at Frogs' Gutter, having returned there on other occasions a hundred times before. So familiar are they with the moor and so well do they like it that there is no longer any scare attached to their getting out of sight, at least not at this time of year. Later on the possibility of a migratory urge would hold some small threat to their old-established habit.

I waited for the moment when Genghis would swallow his last mouthful. When that came he raised his head and looked me full in the eye. I feared it might be to say 'Thanks for the food, now I must fly,' but though the wind of freedom blew over him he took no heed of it and continued to sit on my fist. I held the hood up to his head and he did not flinch, so I slipped it on and held him up for the people to see.

As we came over the hill, and the cluster of cottage and out-houses with its ring fence of stunted, twisted trees came into view, a falcon sailed out from somewhere within its shelter to meet us, and Robert called Infanta down to his lure. We waited while he took her up and fed her. Then we continued on our way and before entering the enclosure we halted again to allow him to take her in and put her down on her block in the hedged weathering ground, so that, having disposed of her he could call the other falcon to him, Donna, who was waiting perched on a branch in the one and only tree that had any height in it.

We had not provided for so large a company and ordinarily I would have done nothing to detain the broad mass of them, but this was so extraordinary an occasion that it was just impossible to let them go as if nothing more than an afternoon's hawking had come to an end. 'Tea and buns' it was to be. Of tea there was a store in the cottage, and 'buns' can cover anything that conceivably can be eaten with a cup of tea. At that moment I felt a deep gratitude to that crowd of people for somehow it seemed that they had been necessary for the gyrfalcon's return. And now their warm good humour linked us all together it was unthinkable not to do everything possible to prolong the happy experience.

I put Genghis in the weathering enclosure with the two peregrines. What an aristocrat he looked by the side of them! Then Robert and I gathered sticks and heather-stalks and crammed them in the fireplace in the cottage living-room, and very soon we had a fire. Through all the crowd and bustle I felt compelled to go outside and see the smoke coming out of the chimney for the first time this year. It made me feel that we were offering up something. We were lighting a beacon to honour Genghis. Fire and smoke. Let the one element praise and magnify its opposite in character—snow and ice! People scattered to bring in more fuel and when the fire was roaring Robert brought a kettle of heroic size out of the kitchen and filled it at the stream which ran outside the kitchen door.

Elbow to elbow we all stood inside the two downstairs rooms amid a roar of talk and laughter enjoying this impromptu tea. Tea-cup in hand I kept pushing around, being anxious to gather as much of the conversation as possible. Everyone had viewed from his own particular angle the gyr's dramatic intervention, and it was interesting to hear the various interpretations of the event from which we were all still a little giddy.

It was raining when we came out. It was so gentle that while we were inside it had arrived unnoticed. Not until we were outside did people exclaim 'It's raining!' The wind had ceased so their surprise was all the greater. The downpour came more as a relief to us than a disappointment, for it was not a sorrowful rain neither was it irrelevant to our mood. During the afternoon our attention had not been allowed to relax, our eyes had strained at the sky and there had been a beckoning from every direction, but now the scene was of a uniform greyness and wetness that drew a curtain over the tumult of the day. People began to go and very soon only our two friends the farmers from the other end of the moor were left behind, and by the time we had taken up the hawks there was nobody in sight beyond the four of us.

When we arrived home Robert and the farmers went directly to the mews to put the peregrines on their perch, and I went into the house to exhibit the returned Genghis. Half an hour later I came out, feeling pleasantly tired, and made my way to the mews with the smell of wet earth for company.

As I went up the incline past the empty weathering enclosure, past the dripping yews, the garden looked more deserted than ever I had known it. And quiet, how quiet everything was! Only two creatures seemed alive in all that world, myself and Genghis.

I went into the mews. On the perch that spanned its length sat the two peregrines, facing me. They never moved, so still were they with heads sunk into hunched shoulders they might have been carved images. Perhaps they, too, were tired. Perhaps the only life that now burned in them was the sleeping memory of the scores of miles they had flown this day. I unwound the leash from my glove, unhooded Genghis and put him on the perch for the night.